Praise for *The P*

"*The Parallel Entrepreneur* is to B2B startups as *Rich Dad Poor Dad* is to real-estate. It's a manifesto to entrepreneurs that you don't need to raise venture capital to build a profitable business; that you can be your own boss; that you can control your own destiny—and still be successful. Ryan is one of the few folks who've successfully navigated this path, and in this book he shares his hard-won experience. If you are thinking about starting a business to generate some cash, you owe it to yourself to read *The Parallel Entrepreneur*."

— **JON MILLER,** CEO of Engagio and Co-founder of Marketo

"*The Parallel Entrepreneur* is a fantastic resource for anyone who has faced the conundrum of wanting to stay at their current job while starting one or multiple companies in parallel—and my experience at Upwork shows me that a lot of people are trying to do this. Ryan, himself a parallel entrepreneur, describes his best practices as well at those collected from others in a compelling, down-to-earth book that will walk the reader through why and how to become a parallel entrepreneur."

— **STEPHANE KASRIEL,** CEO of Upwork

"It's never been easier to start and run a profitable business. That's why I truly believe this is one of the most important books of the modern era workforce. A workforce in which everyone is looking for passive income and work-life balance. Ryan's book is the first one I've seen that perfectly sums up how to do it the right way."

— **MAX ALTSCHULER,** CEO Sales Hacker and SUTRA,
Author of *Hacking Sales* and *Career Hacking for Millennials,*
Investor/Advisor to over 50 tech companies

"*The Parallel Entrepreneur* is about being both an entrepreneur and venture capitalist. In this book, Ryan outlines a simple but effective path to becoming a successful parallel entrepreneur by building multiple businesses simultaneously."

— **TAE HEA NAM,** Founding Managing Director of Storm Ventures
and Coauthor of *Survival to Thrival*

THE PARALLEL ENTREPRENEUR

HOW TO START AND RUN COMPANIES WHILE KEEPING YOUR DAY JOB

RYAN BUCKLEY

To Melissa, Lily, and Norah.
We make a great team.

CONTENTS

ABOUT THE AUTHOR

I HAVE ALWAYS ENJOYED DOING a lot of things at once. In high school, I was one of the kids that tried to do it all. AP classes (I took them all except Physics), music (I was in choir and jazz band all four years), leadership (I was senior class president), and sports (well, actually I didn't do any sports).

In college, at the University of California, Berkeley, I found a way to triple major in four years with economics, environmental economics, and environmental sciences, but decided that was unnecessary. Instead, I graduated with just a bachelor's in Environmental Sciences and a bachelor's in Economics with one semester to spare. That last semester I took acting, music, and Latin. I earned a 4.0 including one A-plus; it was my favorite semester at Cal.

A few years later, I was able to get a master's in public policy at Harvard University and a MBA at MIT simultaneously. There were four of us in the dual Master's program at Harvard and MIT that year so I decided to do something different: I started a business.

That business was Scripped: one of the first online screen-writing applications to make waves in Hollywood. It eventually attracted 80,000 screenwriters, which might have been 80% of the screenwriting population at the time.

The problem was it didn't make enough money, so I launched more businesses. I built a web development consultancy for governments, a mobile campaign donation canvassing app, and a product to help bartenders fill pitchers of beer. I sold my stake in the government consultancy for $5,000 and bought a couple of nice road bikes. The other businesses petered out.

Scripped almost died too, but we were able to pivot the business into the growing content marketing field and raised $18 million dollars of venture equity and debt to rapidly expand it. We renamed the business Scripted and against all odds it is still alive and well today, seven years later.

In the midst of that turmoil, I did what I do: I built another business. This time in the sales technology market. I called it Toofr, named after one of the characters in *30 Rock*.

Toofr was a clever way to find business email addresses, and I decided to do all of the coding, design, and marketing myself. No business partners or investors, just me. It launched in early 2013 and within three years it was paying me more than my day job.

Toofr was always a side business. I kept my day job with Scripted because Toofr didn't require more than an hour of attention per day, and I could easily manage it after hours. Even after I started a family, Toofr kept humming along: paying off my graduate school debt and helping us save for a house in the pricey San Francisco Bay Area.

You don't need to be superhuman like Jack Dorsey or Elon Musk and run multiple public enterprises at once. This book is about how the rest of us can leverage parallel processes to change our lives and find financial freedom.

My objective is to share what I've learned, the patterns I've found in the way that others have done it, and lay down a framework so that you can do it faster and better than the rest of us.

INTRODUCTION

I RECEIVED THIS EMAIL FROM a talented young entrepreneur a month or so after I interviewed him for a marketing position at Toofr, the sales tech website I built and is my main source of income today.

> *Hey Ryan,*
>
> *I wanted to reach out in hope for some advice. I'm inspired by Toofr. It's such a simple service, yet so valuable to your customers, and highly profitable in proportion to the time spent to manage it. I want to create something like this for myself.*
>
> *I would like your advice on:*
> - *How I can build a product that is just good enough to get a first customer.*
> - *How to market and sell without hiring sales people or buying ads.*
> - *How to retaining my customers for as long as possible.*
>
> *Can you offer me any advice?*
> *Regards,*
> *TN*

It was a moment of pure, blazing coincidence. I had just finished this book when he emailed me out of the blue. It's like I wrote it just for him, so I sent him an early draft of my book in response.

Building a product on the internet is relatively easy these days. It's the making money part that's hard.

I know because I've done it, and unlike a lot of entrepreneurs I know, I've done every part of it myself. I code, sell, market, and even file taxes. I learned it all on the spot.

I wrote this book to help you and people like TN become parallel entrepreneurs faster than I did, and to encourage you to do so while you have the safety net of a day job.

In writing this book, I interviewed dozens of entrepreneurs who have done it more successfully than I have. These entrepreneurs have at least two income streams generating $10,000 per month, and they've developed their companies both solo and with a team.

I've divided this book into two parts: Theory and Tactics.

The Theory section will cover all sides of parallel entrepreneurship and lean on both my experiences and those of others who have also ventured into parallel entrepreneurship.

I lay out a framework and incorporate insights and patterns from dozens of parallel entrepreneurs, so that we can understand the rationale behind splitting your time across multiple ventures instead of focusing on just one.

This is important because we've all heard the refrain, "Focus, focus, focus." I'll explain why this is *right* (each business you start should be singularly focused) and why this is *wrong* (because—and this is the point of the book—you can have multiple singularly focused businesses!)

The Tactics section covers everything you need to know in order to plan, build, and run a business on the internet—all while keeping your day job.

This book will not help you open a restaurant or a consulting company. You probably can't keep a day job and start one of those types of businesses. It focuses on internet software businesses because they are what I know and also the most scalable kind of ventures. These are the types of business you can run just at night and on weekends, and you can run several of them at once.

If your goal is to own a website that makes money while you sleep, allows you to (eventually) work one-hour days, and nets you more income than your peers in full-time jobs, then read on.

You can do it if you work hard and get just a little bit lucky.

If your goal is to build a multinational enterprise, list your company on the NASDAQ, and make $100 million dollars, then I'm sorry, this book is not for you. The decisions you'll make, the investment you'll need, and the ability to build a portfolio of your own small businesses are incompatible with the methods described in this book.

The businesses I'm focusing on are singles and doubles, not home runs and grand slams. The businesses I want you to build are little money makers with no staff. Combine them together and you'll be financially free.

Throughout this book I'll explain why keeping your businesses small and simple is very important.

Furthermore, I focus solely on businesses that sell to other businesses. These are called "B2B" companies. I think it's too hard to build a consumer-facing ("B2C") business on your own.

You need scale for B2C to work, and to get scale, you need investors. Yuck.

If you're reading this book, you're probably interested in working for yourself. If you take outside capital, you're also taking on a boss, reporting requirements, and a business partner.

Trust me, unless you need $100 million in your bank account, the investor baggage is not worth it. If you want to raise money and report to a board of directors, then this book isn't for you.

My bias toward B2B business is a direct result of my experience building B2B companies. In fact, I've never built a B2C product, but I have some friends who are successful at it. I have seen and heard directly from these friends that B2B opportunities will get to profitability faster and with less work than B2C counterparts, so that's what I'm promoting here. I want to be upfront about that.

If you need to build something that thousands or millions of people will use, then I'm sorry, this book also isn't for you.

Instead, you'll get helpful resources from my journey along with insights into the nasty pitfalls you'll inevitably discover. This book is designed to be both a story and an encyclopedia that you can keep referring back to as you build your businesses.

I must warn you: what you're about to embark upon is all-consuming, painful, and frustrating. You will want to quit several times before you finally turn your idea into a personal ATM machine.

I wanted to shut down Toofr at one point. I was on the cusp of shutting it down in early 2014. I'm glad I didn't. That would have been a million-dollar mistake! You might find yourself in the same situation, so I've written about that too.

Most importantly, I want you to know that when your monthly revenue from your side income matches your paycheck, the feeling is incredible. It's freedom, it's validation, and it's worth every minute of the struggle!

I hope you stick with it long enough to get there.

In short, this is the book I wish I had access to ten years ago when I was diving into my first company with dreams of starting many others. It would have saved me a lot of time.

And time, my friends, is everything.

Ryan Buckley
Sonoma
December 2017

THEORY

"Give me six hours to chop down a tree
and I will spend the first four sharpening the axe."

—ABRAHAM LINCOLN, 16th President of the United States

"Mastering others is strength.
Mastering yourself is true power."

—LAO TZU, Chinese philosopher

EVERY ENTREPRENEUR I KNOW STARTED with an itch they couldn't scratch. A tiny voice in their head that kept getting louder and louder until one day they could no longer ignore it.

Something needed to be done.

Every person I know who wanted to start a business and didn't pull the trigger had the same set of hesitations.

"I'd love to quit my job but can't right now."

"There are too many competitors."

"I don't have time."

"It's too expensive."

You may have had these thoughts yourself. It's not unusual to be intimidated and conjure up every excuse why you can't do it: you're not prepared, your idea isn't good enough, or you're too busy with work and family.

The fact is, like starting a family, it will never be the perfect time to start a business. You'll never be completely prepared and you won't have every skill needed in advance to run your business successfully.

But fear not! You'll pick up the skills and insights you need to be successful along the way. And timing? Well, that's the main point of this book.

The best time to start a business is now. *Right now.*

The first part of the book, Theory, will explain why this is true.

What Is Parallel Entrepreneurship?

Meet Cornelius Vanderbilt

YOU CAN'T GET MORE PARALLEL than railroad tracks.

Cornelius Vanderbilt became famous as a railroad tycoon, but he built his first fortune in shipping. He owned both shipping and railroad companies until the age of 70, when he sold his last ship and focused solely on railroads.

Born poor, he quit school at age 11 and became the wealthiest person in all of American history. His fortune in today's money would be over $220 billion dollars. That's more than Bill Gates, Mark Zuckerberg, and Warren Buffett combined.

His first business was a ferry service between Manhattan and Staten Island, where he was born. It was while sailing in the waters around New York in the early 1800s that he earned the nickname "The Commodore," which stuck with him throughout his life.

Vanderbilt quickly found additional income streams. He entered the goods trade with his father, and worked as a captain for another entrepreneur in the ferry business who taught him how to run a complex business and fight in the courts to expand his market.

For a decade, he worked a day job as a ship captain while building his own side businesses. Finally, at age 35, he went full-time into his side projects. The scope of those side projects, now his sole focus, would expand enormously.

Vanderbilt noticed that ferries and steamboats were just one piece of a larger freighting ecosystem. The booming cotton economy drove expansion of rail lines between the Southern states and New England, where his ships connected to railroads at ports all along the Eastern Seaboard.

Seizing this opportunity, Vanderbilt began to take over the railroads too. The railroad business led to other opportunities that didn't exist at sea: real estate. He bought large tracts of land in Manhattan and Staten Island to protect and expand his railroads, further increasing his influence and wealth. He bought shipyards and passenger steamboats, and consolidated his railroad companies into the first giant corporation in America.

Vanderbilt was an extraordinary parallel entrepreneur, one of many whom we will study in this book.

Indeed, parallel entrepreneurship is nothing new. Among internet entrepreneurs today, parallel entrepreneurship is discussed at conferences, on podcasts, and in many other business books. It's most commonly referred to as "side hustling." Google that and you'll see there's already a lot of people talking about it.

The unique thing about parallel entrepreneurship today is that it's easier than ever to do it online, and you don't need to stick with traditional side businesses like real estate investing, consulting, and producing online courses. You can have an e-commerce business on the side. You can even have a modern software subscription business (a.k.a. "SaaS business") as a side hustle.

In fact, you can build not just one internet business but multiple internet businesses while still keeping your day job.

The main difference between you today and Vanderbilt 200 years ago is that you don't need to be rich to build a software company. You don't need a huge team, massive servers, and a Ph.D. in computer science to become a software tycoon. You can do it all from your couch with a bowl of popcorn and your favorite Spotify station playing in the background.

From trash to treasure

I didn't start out as an internet entrepreneur. I got my first taste of entrepreneurship while picking up trash in high school.

I've always had an environmental bent. I remember riding up into the Sierra Nevada Mountains in my grandpa's white Toyota pickup truck feeling a twinge of anger every time I saw a logging truck rolling down the highway in the opposite direction with a pile of pine logs in tow.

I didn't know what else to do so I reacted the way any eight-year-old might react. I stuck my tongue out at them. Each and every one. If my grandpa noticed, he never said anything.

Back at home in the San Francisco Bay Area, I sketched imaginary machines that would suck down and store greenhouse gases underground. These contraptions had huge floating fans connected to pipes that ran to buried storage containers and would safely store the carbon dioxide to keep it from escaping.

I had an early interest in science. My freshman year biology class was taught by Mr. Stoehr. As luck would have it, he was also the sponsor of my high school's Environmental Club. I did well in his class and started going to Environmental Club meetings every week, befriending the student leadership and getting to know Mr. Stoehr ("Greg") on a first-name basis.

I made a name for myself by deciding to tackle the littering problem at my school. This too harkens back to those summers spent with my grandpa. He'd never walk by a piece of trash without picking it up and stuffing it into his pocket, lamenting the laziness of the person who dropped it.

Years later my high school friends would tease me about picking up trash. They would ride their bikes ahead of me, call out my name, hold up the 7-11 Slurpee they'd just finished and drop it. Without fail, I'd groan and pick it up, carrying it with me until we came upon the next trash can.

There was a lot of litter at Los Altos High School. I'd see it in the bushes, under the covered hallways, even around the bases of the many trash cans on campus. It drove me crazy!

I was able to recruit two other guys to help me pick up trash every Wednesday after school. We called it "Mission: Trash Pickup," and for the better part of three years we met and picked up trash every week after school.

Needless to say we didn't get a lot of attention from the girls on campus, but the custodians sure loved us. They bought us our own green rolling trash bin that we branded with a spray-painted "MTP." That trash can, which we called the "MTP-mobile," was my first brand, my first logo, and the first thing I ever started and got people to join.

A couple of years later I was invited to participate in a new community service program that my high school was launching. Mrs. Beman, the leader of this new program, asked if I'd like to include MTP in the list of volunteer activities. I agreed but worried that no one would choose our program. It took a special kind of person to choose to pick up trash. How many of us could be out there?

I was happily mistaken. I convinced a few dozen people to choose my activity and sent them all around the school to pick up litter. When we were done the campus never looked so clean.

I learned later that the main draw of MTP was not the elation of seeing a litter-free campus. They picked MTP because they were forced to choose something and they didn't want to get onto a bus and travel anywhere.

That too proved to be an important lesson in entrepreneurship. Sometimes you can't predict demand.

I began my senior year of high school as senior class president and co-president of the Environmental Club. Looking back, this was my first brush with parallel entrepreneurship.

I wanted to take both responsibilities seriously and figured I could manage it because there were no conflicts of interest. Nothing I would do with the Environmental Club would detract from the important responsibilities of a senior class president, which above all else was organizing the prom and fundraising to get ticket prices as low as possible.

I found ways to play both jobs off of each other. I used the familiarity I got with the high school administration as class president to organize an Earth Week that coincided with the national Earth Day 2000 festivities. As class president I also had access to the display case near the main office. One week I filled it with all the litter that MTP collected. Stapled to the wall, using pieces of trash that my fellow students had dropped, I spelled out, "We can do better."

Likewise, the seniors benefited from my improved organizing skills, respect from school authorities, and admission to the University of California. My admission essays were all about my parallel entrepreneurship experiences. So after I received my acceptance letter I was able to focus full time on organizing the senior prom (which we held at a science museum in San Francisco, obviously) and it was awesome!

That prom turned out to be the highlight of my high school experience. Right up there with the custodians buying me a rolling trash can.

Some nerdy, introverted people like me don't enjoy high school. But I thrived. I didn't know it then but I'd already discovered the many varied benefits of parallel entrepreneurship.

Taken after I graduated, it's the only picture I have
of the "MTP-mobile"

Don't quit your day job and then build a startup

Don't quit your job to build a startup. Build a startup and *then* quit your day job. Or keep it and treat it like another income stream. It's totally up to you. That's the big idea here.

One of my favorite parallel entrepreneurs, Marcia Kilgore, says, "You don't give up your day job because you think that your side hustle or whatever it is is going to actually pay off. You always do two things at the same time because one of them may not work, and you want to make sure that you've got another one."

There's no reason anymore to go full-time into any one thing. If you have the itch to try your hand at starting a business, then you should do it while your employer limits your risk with a regular paycheck.

The thing a lot of people seem to forget is that you can start, run, and grow a real business that makes a meaningful amount of money just by working during nights and weekends.

It does mean some amount of sacrifice. You won't be able to do this and keep up with the latest Warriors trades and *This Is Us* episodes.

Still, it's worth the sacrifice. Here's why.

It's getting harder and harder to do traditional Silicon Valley fundraising. The bar is so high that by the time you actually checked all the investors' boxes you wouldn't need their money anymore. When you're a new entrepreneur the finance guys need to de-risk as much as possible, and they do that by expecting you to be flawless.

Similarly, it's getting harder and harder to earn revenue. Customers are getting harder to grab because starting internet businesses is getting easier. Simply put, there's more competition.

At the time of this writing, I've launched six web applications in the last 12 months. Of those six, only two are making money. I support my family primarily with one of them. With every new project I start, I'm grateful to have even one business that works.

It took three years of nights and weekends to get my side business to a point where I can live comfortably off of it. When I launched it, though, the market for online businesses was much less saturated. These days it might take longer to yield the same result, but it's still possible.

You need more than one source of income

Having multiple income streams is the ultimate insurance. It's the same idea that financial fund managers use. It's always better to diversify your investments. Don't be all in on tech stocks or bonds or index funds. You should mix high risk and low risk investments whenever possible.

Think about it. Investors don't move their money serially. They don't go 100% into stocks, then 100% into bonds, and then move everything into some other instrument.

Not even close. They hold a mixture of all of these securities simultaneously. In parallel. Spread across multiple markets and in businesses of different sizes and risk profiles.

In short, the portfolio theory simply suggests you should not be a serial entrepreneur with 100% of your entrepreneurial time invested in one business. You should diversify and be a parallel entrepreneur instead.

I go a step further and suggest that you should do the same with your career. You don't need to rely on a spouse or partner to have the stable or high-risk job. You can have them both by yourself. You can have a low-risk day job and high-risk startup without sacrificing anything from either one.

Parallel entrepreneurs start businesses all at once

Serial entrepreneurs start one business after another. Parallel entrepreneurs start them all at once. It's not for the faint of heart, but the rewards are tremendous.

One of the most successful and prolific parallel entrepreneurs I know is Jonathan Siegel, author of *The San Francisco Fallacy*, co-founder of RightSignature, and owner of Xenon Ventures. When I asked him about parallel entrepreneurship, he lamented that he talks to "fallen angels" every day. These are entrepreneurs who raised anywhere from $4 to $40 million and their companies didn't work out. They didn't necessarily do anything wrong. As we'll see in this book, building a business is hard and a lot of it is unpredictable.

These entrepreneurs had to fully invest 100% of their time into one company while the people who invested in them got to spread their money across dozens of investments. The investors aren't surprised when a business they invested in fails. The entrepreneurs, on the other hand, are stunned. Some never recover.

Starting a business is risky because it takes a lot of time and at least a little bit of capital, and it may take years before you know if it will pay off. There will be a lot of noise along the way, and indicators that you're failing faster or soaring higher than you really are. It just takes time until the ultimate arbiter of truth—cash in the bank—shows its pretty face.

Until then, you keep toiling away, losing out on the low-risk paycheck you might get from a day job or a higher-yielding opportunity that you set aside in favor of the business you've already started.

You're an entrepreneur. You have a million ideas, but you have to pick *just one* of them and then fully commit to it.

Or do you?

Actually, there's no rule saying you can't do more than one small business at a time. There's no physical constraint preventing it.

Look at it this way. You can work a day job and be married, have kids, get a pilot license, binge watch *Game of Thrones*, and play on an intramural softball team. That's pretty normal to do outside of your day job.

So why can't you also start a business? Or two? Or three? If you can have a personal life outside of your day job, why can't you have a professional life outside of your day job too?

The answer, of course, is you can do both. Some of the greatest entrepreneurs of our time are parallel entrepreneurs.

What if Elon Musk had to choose between Tesla, SpaceX, and The Boring Company (his enterprise devoted to digging tunnels)? What if Jack Dorsey decided not to start Square, his payment company, while he was still at Twitter?

We'd all be worse off if these guys decided not to be parallel entrepreneurs because they believed it violated some mysterious unwritten rule that you can't start and run multiple companies at once.

Musk and Dorsey are exceptional businessmen. They've made accomplishments at the highest levels, higher than I will ever reach, and the extent of their successes actually contradicts a lot of what I suggest in this book.

But that's okay. Let's not compare ourselves to the superhumans among us. My point is, the path has already been paved not only by Musk and Dorsey but also by a thousand others like myself who are not brand-name entrepreneurs.

The theories, tools, and techniques are proven and available. Now come on. Let's go.

There's work to be done!

MARCIA KILGORE
Bliss, Beauty Pie, Soap & Glory, FitFlop

I learned about Marcia Kilgore on the "How I Built This" podcast published by National Public Radio. Her story is incredible.

Raised by a single mother in a rural Canadian town, Marcia decided at a young age to earn her own money. She worked hard and was accepted to Columbia University in New York, where her sister lived and worked as a model.

Unfortunately, Marcia wasn't able to make her tuition payments and never attended Columbia as full-time student. Instead, she earned money providing personal fitness training while taking classes at NYU at night. She noticed her skin health deteriorating, and one fateful day Marcia went to get an expensive facial. She had a terrible experience. This was the unlikely event that set in motion her career as a parallel entrepreneur.

After taking a crash course in skin care, Marcia started giving facials to her sister's model friends in her apartment. She maintained her personal training practice too, working those gigs in parallel with her growing skin care business.

Word of her outstanding facials spread and a couple of years later, in 1993, she opened her first small office. In 1996 she expanded into a first three-room spa and named it Bliss. Three years after that, in 1999, Marcia sold Bliss to Louis Vitton. She stayed through the acquisition and remained for a couple of years after Louis Vitton sold Bliss to Starwood in 2004.

Marcia took some time off and in 2006 launched Soap & Glory, a distributor of affordable designer cosmetics. The following year, while still running Soap & Glory, Marcia launched FitFlop, a shoe designed to properly align your body ergonomically as you walk.

Marcia sold Soap & Glory in 2014 to Boots, a large department store in the United Kingdom. She continued to launch more businesses, building Soaper Duper in 2015 and Beauty Pie just last year, in 2017.

Today Marcia is actively working on FitFlop, Soaper Duper, and Beauty Pie. This is parallel entrepreneurship executed to perfection.

Marcia Kilgore
Bliss // Beauty Pie // Soap & Glory // FitFlop

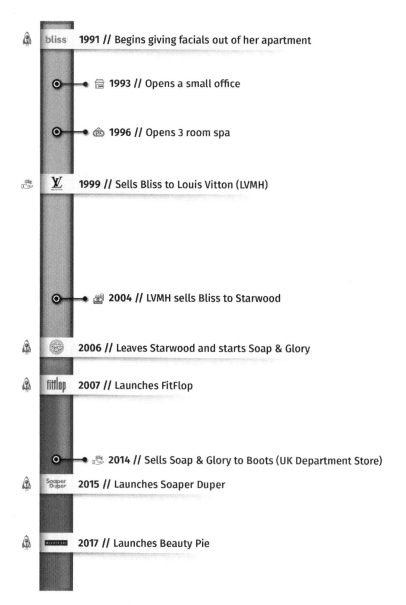

1991 // Begins giving facials out of her apartment

1993 // Opens a small office

1996 // Opens 3 room spa

1999 // Sells Bliss to Louis Vitton (LVMH)

2004 // LVMH sells Bliss to Starwood

2006 // Leaves Starwood and starts Soap & Glory

2007 // Launches FitFlop

2014 // Sells Soap & Glory to Boots (UK Department Store)

2015 // Launches Soaper Duper

2017 // Launches Beauty Pie

2

Personal Rationale

IF YOU READ THIS THEORY section in its entirety and follow the simple rules, I can't imagine why you'd regret giving this a shot.

If your business doesn't take off, you'll have lost time, maybe some money, but gained it back tenfold in new skills and shareable experiences. You'll probably also meet some incredible people along the way.

Parallel entrepreneurs like to find and help each other. Once you put yourself out there, you'll see.

Here are seven reasons to be a parallel entrepreneur. I'll cover each of them in detail.

1. **Develop new skills so you de-risk your career.** There's a price to pay for specialization. The more skills you have, the easier it will be to weather a major economic shift.

2. **See the forest and the trees**. You'll see your day job through a new lens when you spend time working on something else.

3. **Explore a new career**. If you're not sure your current job is right for you, dip your toe into a new career by exploring a side project while you maintain the comfort of your regular paycheck.

4. **Pursue a passion**. If the skill you develop in your side project isn't marketable, that's okay too. Do it if you enjoy it.

5. **Make yourself more marketable for transfers**. You may find a new career within your current company. That's also an accomplishment, and the fastest way to get there is to teach yourself those skills by running a side business.

6. **Structure your evenings and become more productive**. Side businesses force you to use your time wisely. This skill will help you in all aspects of your life.

7. **Gain financial leverage**. You can also start a side business simply for the extra money. When you don't need someone else to sign your paychecks then and only then can you call your own shots.

1. Develop new skills so you de-risk your career

In *Rich Dad Poor Dad,* Robert Kiyosaki writes, "The most important specialized skills are sales and marketing." He mentions this several times throughout his best-selling personal finance book.

Most people don't get the opportunity to develop sales and marketing skills. They're too busy running something, whether it's an Excel spreadsheet, an espresso machine, or a research project. That's what most jobs are: a narrow set of activities in which you entrench yourself throughout your career. You become specialized. The problem with specialization is that your skills may not transfer very well when you lose your job.

It should therefore be no surprise that the most common reason people become parallel entrepreneurs is to develop a new skill set and de-risk their careers. More than two-thirds of the individuals I interviewed gave this response.

The first thing you'll discover as you dive into starting your business is the sheer breadth of skills needed. I started Toofr because I wanted to learn web software development. I didn't know that it would also improve my writing, digital marketing, and public speaking skills.

The more time you spend starting and running your own business, the more professional "merit badges" you earn. The more merit badges you earn, the more valuable you become, both inside and outside of your day job.

So rather than paying for classes at a community college or quitting your job to join an incubator, use your current paycheck to finance your entrepreneurial ambitions. Use your current paycheck to give you the freedom you need to learn and build.

This way you can work for years to build your business on the side and build a great foundation all while benefiting from the security of a full-time job.

Don't feel guilty about it, either. The skills you'll develop on this journey will benefit your employer too.

Rapid new skill development is the top reason to start a new company while you're already working full-time.

You might be surprised to find that the most common set of skills that parallel entrepreneurs have isn't coding and product development. It's writing blog posts and building and analyzing financial statements and models.

Roughly one-third of parallel entrepreneurs I interviewed know how to query a database. If that's not something you want to learn, that's okay. You don't have to. Even fewer can build a website application themselves.

Every single one of them can write their own blog posts, though. Most could write their own ebooks. Nearly two-thirds are comfortable enough with Excel and financial software to build revenue and financial models to use to run their businesses.

Those financial skills are the most common and arguably the most valuable to your business. You can outsource the book-keeping and financial statement development but you can't outsource the ability to understand your own business quantitatively. If you don't have that skill now, it's something you can learn. Take an online course or ask a friend who knows how to use spreadsheet software. Regardless of where you ultimately land, whether it's at your own company or someone else's, a working knowledge of Excel or Google spreadsheets will make you more valuable, increase your salary, and improve your ability to succeed.

These are skills you need. If you don't have them already, a great way to learn them is by trying to set your own entrepreneurial destiny.

2. See the forest and the trees

The counterargument to "focus, focus, focus" is that myopia can sap creativity. More commonly, you'll "miss the forest for the trees."

Sometimes you need to take a few steps back and take the long-range view in order to see your business in a new way and gain valuable, game-changing insights.

I've found that the best way to do that is to have another professional project running simultaneously. Toggling back and forth between projects is a great way to force yourself out of your old way of thinking. When you have to change contexts and wrap your mind around a completely different business problem for a few hours, you'll find that you'll see the first problem in a completely different way.

To illustrate this point, I'll tell you about a very important business model change we were considering for Scripted, my investor-backed marketplace for written content.

I really wanted Scripted to have a software subscription. This revenue model was just beginning to bring in meaningful income for Toofr, and I knew that Scripted could do even better because of its resources, brand, and my team.

But just mentioning this concept at my office job elicited rolled eyes and raised eyebrows.

Everyone was either a nay or an abstention on this one. I couldn't get a single ally. It was a touchy subject because the implications were huge. Everyone was right about that. A subscription model would change every part of our business and make some teams obsolete. It also would sink our revenue temporarily while the subscriptions grew.

At the time, Scripted made money by taking a large percentage of the marketplace transaction between businesses that purchased writing and the writers who sold it. Often this high transaction fee rubbed people the wrong way.

If we moved to a software subscription model we could lower that transaction fee by eighty or ninety percent! I knew this is what our customers wanted, but I couldn't convince anyone that it made business sense.

Yes, it might cannibalize our other revenue. Yes, it might upset the sales reps. (I was sensitive to this because I managed the sales team at the time, but I wanted to try it anyway.) Yes, it could lower our average revenue per user and throw our unit economics out of whack.

I still advocated for the flexible, month-to-month subscription model because I saw that our traditional sales-driven enterprise approach was not working. Our customers didn't want to purchase our writing with lengthy, verbose contracts. The customers who signed, and we did get a lot of signatures, would not renew. The numbers were telling the story but my team didn't want to change.

I said in meetings that not giving our customers what they wanted was wrong. We had to listen to them and then figure out how to make it work. Conversation would ensue, and the conclusion would always be made that my idea was too risky, would create too much change, the board would never approve it, and that we shouldn't give up on the *status quo* yet.

One afternoon, in the midst of all of this, I was sitting in a conference room with our product manager. We had just gone through another grueling series of meetings debating the features and pricing for our newest contracts. We looked at the whiteboard full of notes and I said, "I promise you, we're eventually going to be a simple monthly subscription company. It's going to happen."

Then he laughed. I laughed too. We both laughed. Sadly, when we shifted to the monthly subscription model a few months later, he was one of the guys we had to lay off.

Eventually I was able to convince our stakeholders of the wisdom of the subscription model. Today, Scripted is stronger than it's ever been. Monthly recurring revenue has tripled in the preceding year and the business is profitable.

Moving Scripted to a subscription model was the right move and I have Toofr, my little side project at the time, to thank for that insight.

3. Explore a new career

I'm now in my mid-thirties. My friends are too, and many of them are feeling stuck in careers they chose after college or after graduate school, and they're realizing they're too old to make a switch.

Your thirties are when your income is supposed to accelerate. As my friend and author, Max Altschuler, writes in his latest book, *Career Hacking for Millenials*, "Your twenties are for learning. Your thirties are for earning." You get more raises and promotions in this decade than any other point in your life. Sacrificing that gravy train for a shot in the dark in a new career could be disastrous.

So they stay in jobs they don't like and waft back and forth between numbness and misery. That doesn't sound like a life any of us want to live.

And there's no reason for it. You can have your cake and eat it too!

Let's say you're working in public policy but have always wanted to be an interior designer. You're doing really well at your job. Great boss, great pay, great perks, and you actually like the work, but it's not what you would do if you could choose a career all over again.

What are your options? The **How To Do It** section in this book has the details, but the teaser is simply to just...*do it*. Get immersed, start building a brand, and find the intersection between what you love and what other people need. It will take you some time to find it, so you might as well do it while you're getting paid by somebody else.

Importantly, interior design and public policy have nothing in common, so they work in parallel. Remember that when you work for someone else, you have to maintain a fire wall. When you're working at your public policy job and taking their paycheck, you cannot do *anything* with your side job. You must do it on your free time.

You'll read in the **Staying Out of Trouble** section that keeping your side projects separate from each other is critical. You can't start your own public policy consultancy while you're working at a public policy company. That will eventually create legal friction and backfire.

When you're the owner of both your day job and your side project, you can seek out synergies between the two. We'll cover this distinction with some real examples from the entrepreneurs I interviewed.

Most of the time there's no reason why you can't put the building blocks in place to not just explore a new career, but to start a new business while still getting paid in your day job.

▶ CASE STUDY: John Zimmer, Co-founder of Lyft

John Zimmer studied hospitality management at Cornell. He graduated in 2006 and joined Lehman Brothers in order to get a better finance background, but during the first year of a two-year analyst program he became bored.

When Logan Green, a friend of a friend, posted on Facebook that he was building a carpooling website, John got interested. A course he had taken in college emphasized that overconsumption of resources will ultimately threaten human survival. The lessons stuck with him but he wasn't inspired yet to work on a solution. The carpooling service idea struck a chord.

At the time, Logan was in Santa Barbara and John was working in New York City. The two connected online and met for the first time in person when Logan traveled to New York a few weeks later. They hit it off and decided to collaborate on Logan's idea.

John stayed at Lehman Brothers for another year while Logan built the website and John hammered away on marketing campaigns and partnerships at college campuses. He kept his day job while working on a side project that had no overlap or potential conflicts.

In 2008, when Zimride, the carpooling site, was running and making money, he quit Lehman Brothers.

Friends and family thought he was crazy. "Why would you quit on a sure thing like Lehman?" they'd ask.

Three months later, Lehman Brothers went bankrupt.

As COO of Zimride, John Zimmer is now a major shareholder of a business with 1,500 employees that is worth north of $5 billion.

4. Pursue a passion

Another rationale for parallel entrepreneurship is simply to explore a passion. Since half of the parallel entrepreneurs I interviewed gave this reason for starting a second or a third business at once, I'm going to share two stories.

Josh Pigford is the founder of Baremetrics, a Birmingham-based software company that captured the subscription analytics market by storm. Josh is one of my favorite parallel entrepreneurs. I love his writing and respect his business philosophy.

Since he launched it in 2013, Josh's business has consistently grown about 50% every year. His annual revenue is now over $1.1 million. Not bad for a business that has raised only $800,000 from outside investors and still runs lean with a small team.

Josh's story is particularly interesting during the time prior to launching Baremetrics, when he was essentially a serial parallel entrepreneur. He'd start and stop dozens of businesses, which ranged from consulting projects to software applications. Baremetrics, in fact, was one of those many businesses that Josh was inspired to build back in 2012 and 2013.

It was because of his experience starting and stopping multiple businesses that Josh could tell Baremetrics was different.

"It was like, 'Oh, so that's what it feels like to have something that just works!'" he told me.

Baremetrics, unlike his other ventures, saw immediate fast traction. Soon it consumed all of his time, so he folded his other ventures and for several years was dedicated completely to Baremetrics.

Then, in January 2017, I saw this tweet from Josh:

"I'm launching a super non-digital thing this month: @CedarandSail! Stay in the loop + get 20% off when it launches: http://cedarandsail.com."

The tweet included several pictures of small, geometric plant vases.

Why would the CEO of a hot software startup publicly launch an e-commerce company? I was curious, so I asked him.

He told me it's because he loves the products. He writes on the Cedar & Sail blog, "Separate from business, I make a point to do things that aren't digital…things that require me to use my hands and build actual, real, tangible objects. That manifests itself in everything from gardening to woodworking to electronics to designing home decor."

You don't start a handmade craft business in order to scale rapidly and make a bunch of money quickly. It doesn't work that way. Josh also acknowledged to me that there is no synergy between Cedar & Sail and Baremetrics. None.

But that's what it means to have a passion project. He's not doing it for fortune or fame or any reason other than simply because he loves it, it makes him feel good, and it's an outlet for the roller coaster ride he's on at Baremetrics.

In a previous example I described someone who was working in public policy and was passionate about interior design, so she started a blog. There's a clean, clear line between public policy, which is her day job, and interior design, which is her parallel entrepreneurship project. They have to be separate because of legal consequences with her day job.

Josh's case is different. He's the CEO of Baremetrics and also the CEO of Cedar & Sail. He therefore could blend his projects together a bit, perhaps by selling to the same customers or using the same software. Many parallel entrepreneurs I spoke to scaled up multiple businesses simultaneously by riffing them off of each other.

Again, when you wholly own all the businesses you're working on, you can do that. Josh could have done this too, but instead, he kept them separate simply because he's passionate about building beautiful physical products.

Max Altschuler took a similar parallel trajectory. He's the CEO of Sales Hacker, a media company that hosts conferences on multiple continents and is a fast-growing content destination for information-hungry sales and marketing professionals. He has a small team with revenues north of three million dollars a year.

Let's start at the beginning of Max's career with Sales Hacker. I know it well because I was there.

I met Max via email when he messaged me in late 2012 about a couple of articles I wrote on the Scripted Blog titled "Hacking for Sales." Max was working at the time in Business Development at an online course startup called Udemy.

I filled these posts with programming code to pull names, emails, and other data from public websites that might be useful in email campaigns. He liked them and encouraged me to develop them into a course to host on Udemy. I balked but we became friends and started hosting dinners and meetups with other technology-minded sales people in San Francisco.

The interest grew and Max saw an opportunity to expand our group beyond the handful of regulars and into the broader sales and technology community in the Bay Area. In November 2014 he hosted and organized the very first Sales Hacker Conference. It was magnificent, well-attended in a beautiful theater close to the vibrant North Beach district in San Francisco.

Max sold the tickets, got the sponsors, and lined up the speakers. The rest of us just watched and enjoyed the conference. He would go on to host another conference, and then another, and then he did them in Europe and partnered with other sales training organizations to have smaller meetups similar to the early days of our friendly sales hacker group.

He built a team and the revenue kept growing. Just over four years after launching that first conference he is financially free, traveling to and working from anywhere in the world.

So what would compel him to start SUTRA, a natural, energy-boosting alternative coffee product? It's simple. Passion.

As he put it, "I quit drinking coffee since it was killing me, so I built an alternative."

It's also a pattern in Max's career. When he launched that first Sales Hacker conference he wasn't doing it full-time. He still had a job at another startup as leader of its business development team. And while he was making a lot of money running Sales Hacker, he saw opportunities to invest in sales technology companies and cryptocurrencies. He built several significant parallel income streams.

SUTRA is merely an extension of that trend. He loves the challenge of building a physical product and adapting his many years of hustling in sales and marketing to help SUTRA enter the very competitive beverage market.

I have great respect for Max and Josh. They both founded successful online businesses and passion caused them to throw their hats into the offline ring too. They are true parallel entrepreneurs.

5. Make yourself more marketable for transfers

Taking the policy and design parallel story a bit further, let's say you dove into interior design for six months and either determined that the interior designer market is too saturated or you're just not committed to seeing your new career in interior design all the way through.

But you discovered that you love social media. In the process of immersion, you discovered how to use Instagram and Twitter and interact with strangers in ways you never knew were possible. You then noticed flaws (or just a downright gap) in your employer's social media strategy.

You strike up a conversation with the marketing team at work. You didn't know them before, but now you're friends. It turns out there's budget to bring someone on to manage your employer's social media accounts full time.

You describe what you've been doing in the interior design market, what your ideas are for your employer's accounts, and you get the job.

It wouldn't have happened if you never tried to be a parallel entrepreneur. If you'd never set out to explore, you'd still be wafting back and forth, back and forth, back and forth.

6. Structure your evenings and become more productive

About a third of the parallel entrepreneurs I surveyed were able to keep their day jobs and find time at nights and on weekends to develop other income streams. The most common sources of that extra income are investments like real estate, startups, stock, and cryptocurrencies.

As Kiyosaki suggests in *Rich Dad Poor Dad*, becoming rich is as simple as taking whatever is left after you've paid your monthly bills and putting it into assets that generate cash. You can start by buying stocks. When you've accumulated enough money, you can buy a multi-family house, renovate it, and rent it. And with some good planning and a little bit of luck, in a couple of years you might earn a 50% return and do it again.

At this point you may be able to quit your job or reduce your hours to put more time into your side business. Getting there, though, will require discipline. You will need to structure your non-working hours to maximize productivity. You'll see the best results if you just do a little bit of work each day.

I personally enjoy it. Side hustling means a long, slow grind. You're working all day and then you get home and work into the night. It suits me. I'm not an adrenaline junky. I don't like to drive fast or ski fast or run fast. When I was into road biking I preferred the climbs to the descents. And now when I jog, it's usually with a stroller in one hand and a dog leash in the other. I'm not moving very fast, but a long slow jog is actually my favorite type of workout.

If you love it, it's wonderful. You'll know if you're meant for this path by how long you can sustain that schedule.

Does the extra work *give* you energy or does it sap it from you? Be honest with yourself.

Regardless of the outcome, you'll find that your productivity increases with the amount of structure you put into your day.

And when you're your own boss, you can optimize that structure in the way that works best for you.

7. Gain financial leverage

I saved the most obvious reason for last. You can also start a side business for the money.

Kyle Duck has been an SEO consultant for a long time. I met him last year when I was researching new growth channels for my business. We became internet friends and I became one of his first customers for a new SEO product he launched. It's called Alli AI, and by using it I have dramatically improved the organic traffic to my sites.

Prior to building Alli, Kyle was an SEO and growth consultant. He taught himself software development so he could improve his SEO consulting abilities. He spent a decade consulting and honing his knowledge of SEO, what works, and where the opportunities for automation are hidden. He came up with Alli to streamline his consulting and get financial leverage through passive income.

"I always wanted to build something scalable that I could live on," he told me. "I always wanted to have passive income and develop new skills from growing that income."

With Alli open for business, Kyle is well on his way. He passed $1,000 of monthly recurring revenue (MRR) in his first month after launching, grew to $4,000 the following month and is on track after just four months to break $10,000 MRR. He'll soon have enough passive income flow to focus on building a very large business, which is his ultimate goal. Without funds to hire engineers, Kyle will have to build that business himself, which will take time. His SEO software opens up the time he'll need to build it.

That's the financial leverage I'm talking about. One passive income stream is great. Two passive income streams is much, much better. It means you can sell the first one, liquidate it, pay down your mortgage, and you still have money coming in.

Once you're comfortable with one stream, you don't put up your feet or play golf. Instead, you start another one.

That's the parallel entrepreneur way.

ELON MUSK
Telsa, SpaceX & The Boring Company

I think of Elon Musk as the real-life Tony Stark. The fictional Tony Stark, industrialist wizard by day and Iron Man by night, was a parallel entrepreneur as well.

The breadth and success of Musk's parallel ventures are staggering. He became extremely wealthy at 28 after selling Zip2 for $60 million, a company he had started with his brother just four years earlier. Zip2 was an online yellow pages directory that had morphed into an online publishing portal by the time Compaq purchased it.

Elon did all the original programming for Zip2, a skill he learned on his own by reading books. He used his share of the sale, $22 million, to start X.com, an online bank, which he merged with a competitor to form PayPal in 2000. He wasn't even 30 years old yet. While on his honeymoon a few months later, he was thrown out as CEO. Still believing in the opportunity, he invested more of his own money into PayPal and earned $250 million when it sold to eBay.

This is when Musk started a parallel entrepreneurship path. He launched SpaceX in 2002 after reading about rockets and traveling to other countries to learn about how they're made, bought, and sold. Later that same year, he became interested in electric cars and started meeting the engineers and entrepreneurs who were building them. He actually introduced the founding team of Telsa to each other and made a large investment into their company. He became Tesla's CEO in 2008, two years after co-founding Solar City.

For ten years Musk toiled away as the founder and chief executive officer of two major companies, each facing growing pains and setbacks. Fortune would favor this parallel entrepreneur in the long run, and he has recently expanded his portfolio to include OpenAI, Neuralink, and The Boring Company.

He is prolific, ambitious, and successful beyond comparison. A true decathlete of parallel entrepreneurship.

Elon Musk
Tesla // SpaceX // The Boring Company

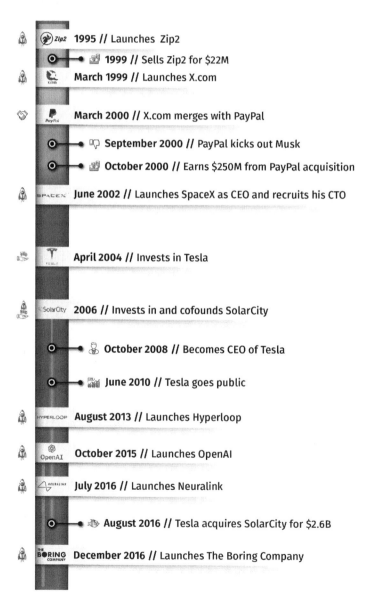

1995 // Launches Zip2

1999 // Sells Zip2 for $22M

March 1999 // Launches X.com

March 2000 // X.com merges with PayPal

September 2000 // PayPal kicks out Musk

October 2000 // Earns $250M from PayPal acquisition

June 2002 // Launches SpaceX as CEO and recruits his CTO

April 2004 // Invests in Tesla

2006 // Invests in and cofounds SolarCity

October 2008 // Becomes CEO of Tesla

June 2010 // Tesla goes public

August 2013 // Launches Hyperloop

October 2015 // Launches OpenAI

July 2016 // Launches Neuralink

August 2016 // Tesla acquires SolarCity for $2.6B

December 2016 // Launches The Boring Company

Business Rationale

THE PERSONAL BENEFITS I DESCRIBED could apply to having just one additional income stream. But I'm arguing for more than that. Let's consider why it's best not to stop at just one. Entrepreneurs and solo founders these days should have several.

You might already be thinking, "Wait a second, I'm supposed to focus on one, maybe two things, and get those to work before doing anything else. And one of those things is my day job."

Sure, a day job and some stocks is a fine way to do things. You can focus on investing and you may get rich, but it won't happen very quickly and your gains could get wiped out during a down market. You could also work hard every day, toiling away for a promotion while you build someone else's generational wealth and you get what's left over.

I'm not saying it's a bad thing. In fact that's how most people do it. But there is another way.

Instead of tying your wagon to someone else's company (via the stock market and your day job) you can invest in yourself (via new skills) and get equity in your own business at the same time.

Instead of hoping that your first idea turns out to be the best idea, you can test multiple ideas at once, build them, launch them, and even run them for a while. I'll describe this process in much greater detail in the second half of the book.

Instead of banking on one business replacing your day job salary and falling short, you can stack the revenues of multiple businesses until in aggregate you're making more than your old paycheck.

This is ultimately why you should run multiple side businesses at once. It increases the likelihood of success and each new business you add takes less additional time than the last one.

Why Growth Plateaus Happen in SaaS

There is a natural limit on how much money you can make as a solo founder without outside capital.

Given that there is a cap on the income stream from any one business, in order to continue your growth, you'll need to start more businesses. If you can't grow up, you have to grow out.

I've found this to be especially true in the software-as-a-service (SaaS) industry. There are growth plateaus that you hit along the way and they are notoriously difficult to break out of. In fact, you may never break out of them. You may hit one and be stuck there for months or even years.

When that happens you have two options: sell the business or keep it and start a new one.

This has happened to me several times throughout my career in SaaS, both with Scripted and Toofr. In fact, I'm experiencing it right now. Toofr's revenue has plateaued for the last several months and I'm actively working to break through it. It gets harder and harder.

The logic behind why this happens goes like this.

Your subscription software business grows when the increase in new revenue exceeds the decrease in churned revenue. New revenue is just what it sounds like: a new customer signing up for a monthly subscription of your product. They're coming in and paying you for the first time. Churned revenue is the opposite. It's an existing customer cancelling their subscription.

There are also the forces of upgrades and downgrades, but for most businesses those movements are a fraction of the volume, 15% at most, of new and churned revenue amounts. So let's just focus on acquisition and churn.

If you get $1,000 of new subscriptions and lose $250 of existing subscriptions, then you grow $750 in monthly recurring revenue. I'm intentionally not saying how many customers those revenue numbers represent. It could be four customers paying you $250 each or 1,000 customers each paying you $1. For the purposes of sheer revenue growth, it doesn't matter. (I'd argue it's safer to have more customers paying a smaller amount, but let's table that for later.)

The problem every SaaS business eventually runs into is

when churn catches up to acquisition. If you keep acquiring $1,000 of new revenue each month, then inevitably, and I do mean *inevitably*, churn will reach $1,000. And there you'll sit, in limbo land, not growing, not shrinking, until you can do something to reduce that churn (better customer support, fewer bugs) or acquire more revenue (advertisements and promotions, new features).

The reason every business eventually hits this plateau can be explained with basic math. Churn is a relatively constant percentage of revenue. It's very difficult to dramatically change your churn rate and it is influenced by two main factors: the industry you're in (e.g. marketing vs healthcare) and the average customer size (e.g. small business vs enterprise).

Most B2B entrepreneurs will sell to small businesses. Both of my companies sold primarily to small businesses. The nice thing is there are literally millions of them in the United States alone, and millions more worldwide. The bad thing is they churn pretty fast and prefer to be on monthly rather than annual contracts. When you charge someone every month instead of every twelve months, your customer gets twelve more opportunities to churn. Therefore, monthly contracts will always churn at higher rates than annual contracts.

So why not just do annual contracts? Because annual deals have longer sales cycles and involve more paperwork. Your customers will want more diligence, they'll want to try before they buy, and they'll want to customize your contract every time. As solopreneurs, we don't have time for all of that.

That's why I take the higher churn and a faster sale every time.

Here's what higher churn looks like. This chart represents the net monthly growth of a business that adds $1,000 of new revenue every month and churns 10% of existing revenue every month. You can see the drop-off in net new revenue. Within twelve months it falls 75% and drops at the same rate after that.

Within two years if you're still just adding $1,000 of new customers your churn, still at 10% of existing revenue, is $920. You're working harder to get that $1,000 of new revenue (because it always gets harder to acquire new revenue over time) and keeping less than 10% of it.

Ouch. It hurts.

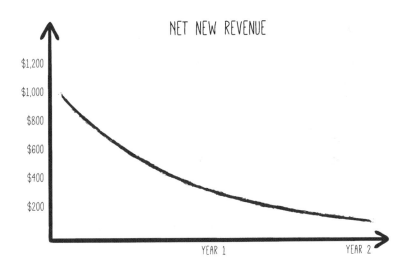

NET NEW REVENUE

On the bottom line revenue side, here's what it looks like. This is what we call a plateau. You're capping out at $10,000 of monthly recurring revenue (MRR). In fact, there's a pretty simple formula you can use to quickly get at this revenue cap:

New revenue / Churn rate = MRR. In this example, that's $1,000 / 10% = $10,000.

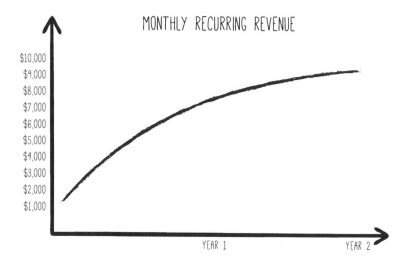

So $10K per month is your upper bound on how much money you'll make with this business. Not bad, but not great. If you want to break past a $120K salary you'll need to think outside the box and either lower your churn or increase revenue.

You have two choices: Go from good to great, which I'll discuss shortly, or build another new box and stack your plateaus.

Stacking Your Plateaus

Parallel entrepreneurship means stacking your plateaus on top of each other. It's admitting that SaaS businesses have an upper bound in MRR and to break out of it you need to hire more people, which may mean taking on debt or equity financing and spending more money on marketing.

You may decide not to do that.

Doubling down on your business means greater risk for an unknown reward. I would assume that at the plateau you're not working very hard. The business is humming along, it's just not really going anywhere. Like I said, not growing, but not shrinking. You're making $10,000 per month and doing very little work.

That's great, congrats! Why mess with that? You have an ATM machine spitting out $330 every day into your pockets. Don't risk losing it. Leave it be. If you want more money, start another business and stack the plateaus.

If you followed this advice and started your second business one year after your first one and it had the same growth parameters of $1,000/mo of new revenue and 10% churn, your *combined* MRR chart will look like this:

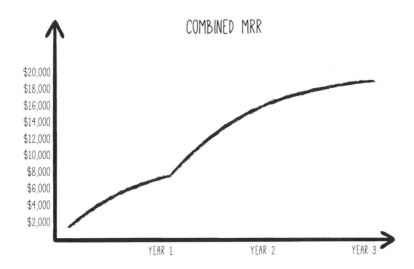

Whether that base plateau is your own business or the salary from your day job, the stacking plateaus concept still applies. That's the business rationale for parallel entrepreneurship.

From Good to Great

If you can get your business up to $10,000 in monthly recurring revenue (MRR), then that's really good. Most entrepreneurs never get there.

It's good but not *great*.

Jonathan Siegel gave me advice that I'll never forget. I use this bit of wisdom to fire up my drive. He says, "Any $10,000 per month business can be a $100,000 per month business." These are crumbs, he says, compared to what the larger companies are earning. The hard growth steps, he argues, happen beyond that first $100,000 per month. Less than that is just discipline and some creativity.

He also argues that if your monthly churn is 3% and your net monthly growth is 4% then you will have a phenomenal business. This Rule of 34 (I'll name this rule on his behalf) is what we should all strive for. You may only get there once in your entrepreneurial career, so to increase the likelihood of doing this, you have multiple businesses running at once.

Finally, a great business has what's known as "net negative churn." This is the holy grail of SaaS businesses, when revenue growth from your retained customer base consistently offsets the revenue lost from cancellations.

To make this point clearer, let's look at this table.

Adds Revenue	Loses Revenue
New customers	Cancelled customers
Upgraded customers	Downgraded customers
Reactivated customers	

Let's say you're adding $1,000 of new customers every month. You're also getting another $1,000 from upgrades and $500 reactivations (customers who canceled and then came back). That's bringing $2,000 of new monthly revenue into your business.

On the flipside, let's say you're losing $500 from cancellations and downgrades each month. This means on net you're adding $1,500 of revenue to your business each month.

Adds Revenue	Loses Revenue
New customers: $1,000	Cancelled customers: $500
Upgraded customers: $1,000	Downgraded customers: $500
Reactivated customers: $500	
Total added revenue: $2,500	Total lost revenue: $1,000

Net negative churn is when, setting new customer revenue aside, you're still adding revenue every month. In this case, you would be making $1,500 from upgrades and reactivations and losing $1,000 from cancellations and downgrades. You're adding $500 each month from *existing* customers.

If you're able to grow a business before you've added a single new customer then you're in *great* shape. You can stop reading now, shut your other businesses down, and focus on that one.

I haven't experienced this yet myself, but I'm working on it. It's why I still have multiple businesses running today.

Exploiting Synergies

Nobody can run a pizza parlor, a nail salon, and a grocery store at the same time. Even the most ambitious local businessperson couldn't do that.

But can you open more than one restaurant? Sure, it happens all the time. I think of Tyler Florence and his restaurants El Paseo in Mill Valley and Wayfare Tavern in San Francisco. Same chef, two different restaurants within a few miles of each other.

Can you open multiple cafes? Absolutely. Look no further than the dominance of Philz Coffee, which began in San Francisco's Mission District and spread throughout the city and then to every corner of the San Francisco Bay Area. (By the way, here's a fun fact: Phil Jaber spent *seven years* perfecting his first blend, Tesora, which means "treasure" in Italian.)

I was delighted when a Philz popped up within walking distance of my house in the suburbs 20 miles outside of the city. It's a perfect example of parallel entrepreneurship applied to brick and mortar businesses.

So what's the difference between running a chain of cafes and running a slough of disparate shops?

It's this word: *synergy.*

Synergy is one of those cliche business terms that gets mocked because it shows up on corporate HR posters and is said around the table in boardrooms. I think it gets an unfair rap. Synergy is a critical concept to embrace if you're going to be a successful parallel entrepreneur.

As Andrej Danko, VP of product at an artificial intelligence studio that builds and runs multiple companies at once told me, "Doing completely mutually exclusive businesses is very hard. There are no economies of scale. You can't leverage IP or operational skills across businesses."

▶ CASE STUDY: Philz Coffee

When you have a busy cafe, some name recognition, and a cult following like the founder of Philz Coffee did, opening the second cafe is a lot easier than opening the first one. Let's take a high-level look at what's required to open a new Philz cafe:

Financial needs
- *Point of sale terminal*
- *Cash transfers and security*
- *Accountant and bookkeeping*

Product needs
- *Coffee supply and storage*
- *Coffee brewing devices*
- *Milk, sugar, honey, and other condiments*
- *Baked goods supply*

Personnel needs

- *Management*
- *Staff*
- *Hiring and training resources*

Marketing needs

- *Grand opening*
- *Ongoing local outreach*

Facility

- *Renovation*
- *Lease*

Looking at the above list, there are both *direct* and *indirect* synergies with the existing cafes. The direct synergies are financial. Phil can use the same point of sale and accounting team. If the second cafe is in the same city then he can also use the same bank for cash deposits.

Product needs are the same. Since Phliz doesn't bake its own muffins, he'll need a new supplier unless they'll distribute out of the city. Same with the coffee roasting. Philz wants only the best, freshest coffee beans (they grind their proprietary blends on the spot) so some supply chain logistics may also be required for coffee beans if the second cafe is too far away.

Indirect synergies are personnel, marketing, and facility needs. Although they won't be exactly the same (they'll need a new location, obviously, and new people) the playbook is the same. If it's not written down then it can be transferred by Phil or one of his first employees at the Mission District cafe.

Let's imagine, for a second, that Phil decided instead to open a pizza parlor. What synergies would he have then?

Very few.

It would be incredibly difficult if not impossible to launch and run a pizza parlor while simultaneously running a cafe. That kind of parallel entrepreneurship is destined to fail.

When you have a profitable and growing SaaS business, it's like having one cafe. The nice thing about cafes is they can get more revenue simply by replicating themselves in another location. But you can't do that on the web. You can't clone a SaaS business in another location (by giving it a new domain name) and expect to double your revenue. That's just not how the internet works.

The internet equivalent to opening that second cafe is to start another SaaS business that is separate from the first profitable one but still benefits from synergies.

▶ **CASE STUDY: Sheel Mohnot**

Sheel Mohnot is another parallel entrepreneur *par excellence*. After selling his online payments business to Groupon, he started Thistle, a food company that delivers sustainable plant-based meals to homes in major cities throughout California. He also runs a podcast, an auction platform, and a financial technology fund within 500 Startups, a prestigious startup incubator with offices around the world.

He does this all in parallel because he's found ways to exploit synergies across his projects, delegate his way out of daily management, and turn his cost centers into profit centers.

Let's dive into Thistle to really see what I mean.

Thistle competes in a very difficult market. Blue Apron, the market leader, went public in June 2017 and its stock price has had a precipitous 70% decline since the public offering. Another major competitor, Plated, sold to Albertsons for $200 million. Other meal delivery services including Sprig, which raised $59 million and was valued at over $150 million, had to shut down.

So what did Sheel do differently? How has Thistle thrived while his well-heeled competitors failed or exited? He successfully approached the problem like a parallel entrepreneur.

First of all, he only raised $1 million for Thistle. He forced his business to run lean, operating profitably from the beginning. Even if you're small, you won't be forced to shut down while you're minting money.

This profitability constraint in turn forced Sheel to be creative. Meal delivery is a complex business, and arguably the hardest part is packaging and delivering meals on time. This cost is often higher than the cost of the food itself. To keep costs down, Sheel found a commercial kitchen that someone else was paying $20,000 per month to use. He negotiated a deal to sublease the kitchen from 9pm to 5am for just $5,000 per month.

Startups that raise gobs of money usually don't make smart decisions like this. Thistle now serves tens of thousands of customers each week and is profitable with 220 employees.

For Sheel personally, he is a co-founder of Thistle but is not the CEO. That gives him the flexibility to run his auction business, a fund in 500 Startups, and other personal investments that generate meaningful monthly revenue streams.

Staying Out of Trouble

THERE ARE FOUR BASIC RULES to follow when you're leading a double (or triple or quadruple) life as an entrepreneur. I'll describe them here.

Rule #1: Unless you own 100% of all of your businesses, you need to maintain a firewall between them.

Your ambitions and assets can be shattered in one swift blow if you don't follow this rule. Never, ever, ever mix your side projects with your day job. That means don't use the same laptop, code snippets, or even the same printing paper. If you think I'm being overkill on this point, think again. I'll illustrate this point using two very different examples from my own career.

Common example: You work for someone else
and have a business on the side

Even though I am a co-founder of Scripted, it stopped being "my" company almost as soon as we launched it. That ownership dynamic shifted when we took in venture capital, hired a larger team, moved into an office, and started really cranking on our growth targets.

Also, I was not the CEO of Scripted until the year before we sold it. So even though I was a co-founder, my day-to-day work life was pretty normal. I reported to the CEO and could have been laid off or fired just like anyone else at the company.

Toofr was running on a nights and weekends schedule on the side, without conflicting with Scripted, except for a daytime phone call or an email here or there. When there was money on the line and I needed to take a call, I'd step out of the office or schedule them on my lunch breaks.

I admit to doing some Toofr support emails in the office, but I did them in the only place it seemed appropriate: on the toilet in the bathroom using my personal iPhone. (For those of you reading this who might have received a Toofr support email from me during this time and are now stuck with that visual, I'm sorry.)

For these phone calls and emails I always used my own iPhone and not the company laptop. Scripted paid a portion of my phone bill because we all used our personal phones for work. Nobody wanted to carry around a separate device just for Scripted, so the company paid roughly half of our phone bills because we figured half the data usage, if not the voice fees, could be work related. Therefore the other half of the bill could be personal, and in this context my Toofr emails and calls were personal. I felt fine with that.

One thing I never did was have a byte of Toofr code on my Scripted laptop. I was paranoid about this. I knew how messy this could get if my relationship with Scripted were to suddenly sour. I couldn't imagine what would cause it, but I knew if it did and Toofr code was found on company property, I could be forced to *hand all of Toofr over to Scripted*. All those long nights of hair-pulling programming would be for nothing.

I had a MacBook Air for work and I loved it. My home laptop was an Asus eePc, a tiny Windows laptop that was awful for programming.

MacBooks are Unix-based, giving you roughly the same environment as a website server. That made it easy to have your local environment mimic your production environment, reducing bugs and setup time.

I couldn't figure out how to make it work on my tiny Windows PC, so my solution was to log into a server and do all my work there. It was annoying but it worked. As tempting as it was to use my Scripted laptop instead, I didn't do it. You shouldn't either.

As soon as I had the money, I splurged on a top-of-the-line MacBook Pro with a 15-inch screen. I spent about $3,000 on it, but after years of hacking on Toofr with a tiny laptop, I deserved it. It's still my main machine. I'm writing this book with it today.

It's been about a year since I left Scripted, and I've been very public about Toofr's success and how much of my time working on it overlapped with Scripted. I've had no problems because I followed my own rules.

Alternate example: You own all your businesses 100%

If you're the sole owner of every business that you're working on and see it staying that way for the foreseeable future, then you have nothing to worry about. Mix and match, share code, paperclips, everything. It's that synergy word again. This is the key to being a successful parallel entrepreneur, actually. To run multiple businesses at once you need to share resources. To share resources, you need to own the businesses fully.

This is what I'm doing now with each of my online businesses. Toofr, Inlistio, eNPS, and Thinbox share a lot of the same code. Everything from front-end templates to back-end subscription libraries are shared and tweaked between them. Why should I write another subscription feature when the one from my other business will work perfectly well? Why design a brand new pricing page when I've already optimized one for my other business?

Same goes with software. I use Sketch to manipulate text and images for banners and remarketing ads. I don't use a separate license for each business I run today.

This is the goal. This is where you want to be. Parallel entrepreneurship gets a lot easier as soon as you're legally able to share resources between the companies you're working on.

As Buddy Arnheim, a partner at the prestigious law firm Perkins Coie reminded me, the caveat is you may ultimately decrease the value of one or both of your companies by obfuscating which company owns which intellectual property (IP). It can be confusing to future investors and acquirers, which will complicate your liquidity prospects.

So before you irrevocably tie your businesses together by sharing critical IP or even trivial code snippets, think it through. Can you easily explain the relationship between your two businesses to someone who wants to put money into just one of them? Can you surgically remove the IP from one if you wanted to sell the other?

The point is to be very clear about what you're doing. Whether or not you fully own both businesses, you need to have clear documentation of the flow of IP.

In fact, even if you're the co-founder and CEO of your day job, as I was at Scripted even while I had Toofr running on the side, you have to be aware of the "corporate opportunity doctrine" or COD.

Stimmel, Stimmel, and Smith, a law office in San Francisco, writes that COD means that a fiduciary (which you would be as an employee or CEO) "can not take for him or herself a business opportunity that should, instead, be reported and given to the company."

In other words, when you're running your side business, you can't take business opportunities away from your day job and funnel them to yourself. It would be like a support engineer offering up a consulting engagement outside of the office to a customer needing help. That kind of business belongs to the employer.

Finally: Do not mix funds

Importantly, even though Scripted actually used Toofr quite a bit, Scripted never paid for Toofr. I gave free accounts to Scripted employees who wanted to use Toofr and did a fair amount of prospecting for Scripted using Toofr myself.

There were real costs for this activity but I never charged for it. Not a single penny. I thought this was really important so whenever I broke up with Scripted there would be no awkward money trail to follow.

And this should be obvious, but if you have access to a charge account or credit card for your day job, never use it for your side business. Not even for a cup of coffee. It's not worth it. Little mistakes like that can change your day job's perspective from "Oh, whatever" to "What a jerk, let's take what's ours."

Inevitably there will be some awkwardness with your previous employer when you're public about your side venture. But if you follow this rule then there will be no reason for them to be upset.

You might even find that they'll be happy for you. That's the goal.

▶ CASE STUDY: Google and Uber

This story, documented all over the internet in 2017, is a study in exactly what *not* to do when you launch a side business.

The case involves a star engineer who worked in Google's self-driving car division, which later spun out as its own company, Waymo. Google alleges that this engineer downloaded 14,000 documents, nearly 10 gigabytes of data, prior to quitting to start his own autonomous vehicle company.

Google claims the stolen documents described Google's proprietary lidar system, the technology that self-driving cars use to "see" the world around them. It's a critical technology and the major companies in this market, including Google and Uber, have each developed their own systems.

That theft alone would be a major issue, but it became a huge problem when Uber acquired the former Google engineer's company a mere six months after he launched it. Google alleges that the stolen documents went with the acquisition, an allegation that Uber denies.

This is what happens when you launch a new business that is competitive with your old employer. It gets really messy really fast.

In February 2018, Google and Uber reportedly settled out of court. Under the reported terms of the agreement, Waymo will receive at least a .34 percent equity stake in Uber, which would be worth around $245 million. Meanwhile, Uber will not use any of Google's intellectual property in its own self-driving efforts. There are a few takeaways for you from this story.

1. Be very careful if you launch a business similar to your day job while you're employed or even shortly afterwards. The law is generally on the employer's side if your new business overlaps in any way. Better yet, don't overlap at all.

2. Never, ever, ever take anything from your employer and use it for your own business. And the worst thing you can do is take intellectual property, as alleged in this Google case. It's a surefire way to get sued.

Rule #2: Your side projects should be very different than your day job.

While I was working at Scripted, I would not have been able to start a marketplace for content managers, or editors, or built an inbound marketing analysis tool, while claiming any of them as a side project, separate from Scripted.

Any of those projects would be way too similar to my day job. Scripted would not have been happy about that. Tables turned, as a Scripted executive if I caught wind of an engineer spinning up an inbound marketing subscription tool on the side, I'd be bothered by it.

There's simply no way to maintain the firewall when your day job and your side business are a similar product, a similar market, or have similar customers.

The details here boil down to the legalese, which I'll get to in the next section, but suffice to say that "intellectual property" is a fairly broad term. When you sign the paperwork at a new job, you invariably sign something called a Proprietary Information and Inventions Agreement.

The "information" part is the tricky part. You may claim that your invention was distinct, that you followed my Rule #1 to the letter, but it will be very difficult to claim a distinction of information. If what you *learn* at your day job is used to *benefit* your side project in material ways, then there's a conflict.

To avoid the conflict, you have a few options:

- **Quit your job**. And when you do, read very carefully what you can and can't do with the confidential

information from your employer. You may need a
cooling off period before you can launch your company.
You don't want to start a new venture only to be
immediately sued by your old boss.

- **Be an intrapreneur.** In other words, start the product
  within your company. Convince the leadership that
  your idea is great, and see if you can get the resources to
  launch it internally. You won't own the product, but you
  can ask for compensation if the new product takes off.

- **Spin it out.** Ask your employer to let you take some IP
  out of the company with you. There is a legal cost here
  and the employer will likely want to keep some equity
  in the spinoff, but this tactic has worked wonderfully
  for many entrepreneurs.

▶ CASE STUDY: iCIMS

My favorite example of a spinoff is by an entrepreneur named
Colin Day. Most people haven't heard of him.

In 1999 Colin was your typical college graduate working at
his first real job. He had landed at a staffing company for IT professionals in New Jersey called Comrise. He woke up, went to
work, and did his job. He was great at it and developed a rapport
with the owner. But when he got home at the end of the day, he
felt something was missing. There was an itch he couldn't scratch.

He channeled that extra energy into writing business plans.

He was looking for an idea that he could quit his job and run with. Then a unique opportunity to land his entrepreneurial dream came from the unlikeliest of places: his boss.

Comrise had recently begun to build a software product for recruiters. Colin was able to convince the CEO to let him quit, take that product with him, and run it as a separate business.

This was nearly twenty years ago when web technology wasn't nearly as inexpensive and available as it is today. Colin would need a significant amount of funding to pay the engineers to complete the project. Because Colin had already proven himself as a trustworthy employee, the CEO provided him with $2.5 million in loans over two years to build it.

Now Colin's business, iCIMS, is one of the fastest-growing private internet companies in the world and makes more than $100 million revenue every year.

Colin made the leap from employee to parallel entrepreneur the right way. Unlike the engineer in the middle of the Google / Uber lawsuit, Colin did everything above board. He didn't sneak around and try to copy the recruiting software. He saw the opportunity, asked permission, and was rewarded for it.[1]

---

1   For more about his story, listen to his interview with Nathan Latka here: http://nathanlatka.com/thetop724/

RICH BARTON
Expedia, Zillow, and Glassdoor

Rich Barton appeared on my radar a few years ago when I saw him speak at a Goldman Sachs conference. He was introduced as the founder of Zillow, Glassdoor, and Expedia. That blew my mind. The same guy did all of that? Indeed, he did. And a lot of it was done in parallel.

Rich started at Microsoft in 1991, a couple years after graduating from Stanford with a degree in engineering. By 1994, Rich sparked the idea for Expedia, suggesting to none other than Bill Gates himself that the CD-ROM travel guidebook they were slated to create should instead be an online destination for booking travel. Gates approved the change and allowed Rich to lead the charge, ultimately launching Expedia online in 1996.

Expedia expanded and spun out of Microsoft with a separate IPO in 1999. It sold four years later for $3.6 billion to InterActiveCorp. Rich took a year off and joined Benchmark, a prestigious venture capital firm, as a partner just as he launched Zillow in February 2005. Two years later, in 2007 while still active with Zillow, Rich co-founded Glassdoor.

According to his LinkedIn profile, today Rich is chairman of each of Zillow Group, Glassdoor, and a new travel website called Trover. He sits on the boards of Netflix and Nextdoor among several

Rich Barton:
Expedia // Zillow // Glassdoor

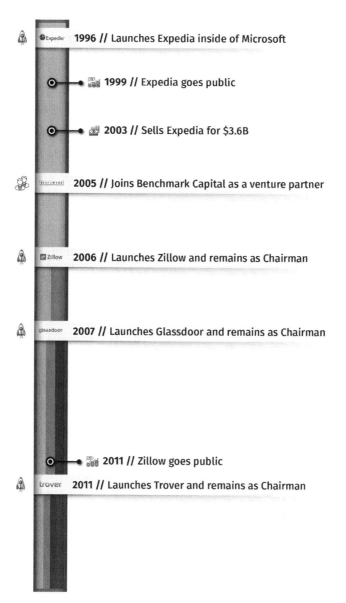

1996 // Launches Expedia inside of Microsoft

1999 // Expedia goes public

2003 // Sells Expedia for $3.6B

2005 // Joins Benchmark Capital as a venture partner

2006 // Launches Zillow and remains as Chairman

2007 // Launches Glassdoor and remains as Chairman

2011 // Zillow goes public

2011 // Launches Trover and remains as Chairman

others. Although not as well-known as Elon Musk and Jack Dorsey, I put Rich's ambition and execution right up there with both of them.

Rule #3: Keep it quiet, but if you're asked about it, don't lie.

Most of my friends knew I was running Toofr while I was working at Scripted. I even did a quick demo of Toofr in the final meeting with one of the venture capital firms who invested in Scripted. The partner loved it and saw it as an indicator that I was the kind of entrepreneur in whom he'd like to invest: scrappy, clever, and able to move fast and build cool things.

Over the years when Scripted and Toofr overlapped, I didn't hide Toofr from view or lie about it. But I also didn't gloat about how much money it was making. For my last two years at Scripted, Toofr generated more revenue than my Scripted salary. Only my wife knew that.

When Scripted employees saw it on my LinkedIn profile, I told them it was a side project, something I worked on to learn how to program, which is 100% true.

It's hard to grow a side business when you can't be very public about it. I never posted about Toofr on my Facebook page and rarely mentioned it on LinkedIn. Toofr had a blog, a Twitter account, and a Facebook company page, so I'd push content up there but did so anonymously.

I also had a newsletter with distribution to nearly 20,000 people who registered for Toofr over the years. I was careful to scrub it for Scripted employees and others in my Scripted universe who may have signed up to explore.

I removed them because I didn't want them to receive a newsletter describing all these new features in the middle of the day and get confused. They wouldn't know that in my newsletters I'd intentionally make Toofr look bigger and busier than it is. I'd also write the newsletter the night before and then use MailChimp to schedule the delivery for the middle of the following day.

I wanted to boost my appearance to the people on my newsletter list, not to the people who were depending on me to help Scripted succeed. Filtering where I could helped avoid unnecessary confusion.

▶ CASE STUDY: Josh Pigford

I mentioned Josh's story earlier. He's the CEO of a hot subscription analytics company who decided to also publicly launch an e-commerce company.

So I asked him if he were concerned about how his Baremetrics customers might perceive his side business. Here's what he told me.

"I address the negative perception by blocking trolls on Twitter and email," he said.

He'll even cancel Baremetrics accounts of customers who are rude to his staff, especially when they blame downtime or other problems that every internet business has on Josh's attention to his side business.

"Everybody has a different way of running a business and staying sane running a business," he told me.

For Josh, Cedar & Sail is a creative outlet, basically a hobby, and he believes that just because his hobby has a website and makes money it shouldn't be treated differently than anyone else's hobby. Some people play pickup basketball. Some people knit, work on cars, or plant a vegetable garden.

Josh has a lifelong habit of turning his hobbies into businesses and he's unapologetic about it. He gives his employees the same opportunity.

"I encourage people on my team to have side projects. One of my customer support guys recently competed on *Master Chef*. He works at a restaurant on some nights. Baremetrics has always had a culture of side projects. I even give feedback on my employees' side projects during our one-on-ones."

It's ingrained into his company's culture and he doesn't pretend to be purely altruistic about it. There are tangible benefits.

"It's a healthy thing to flex new parts of your brain. It comes back and benefits Baremetrics. Doing other projects gives your brain a break or gives a new skill set or perspective that makes Baremetrics better in the long run."

His advice for other entrepreneurs is pretty simple: "The idea that you can't have hobbies is absurd. Ignore those people."

So go ahead. Start a business and keep your day job.

Rule #4: Complete your PIIA and know what it means.

If you included your side projects in the Proprietary Information and Inventions Agreement (PIIA) that you probably signed when you started your day job and followed the three rules above, then you should be fine. It's still important that you understand what a PIIA is and why you had to sign it.

The easiest way to explain a PIIA is from the perspective of your company's founder.

Entrepreneurs don't start their own businesses to lead normal lives. They don't want to go to the office every day, do some work, come home, sleep, and do it all again. No, they want a *pay day*. They want to liquidate that equity and chill out for a while, pay off debts, and maybe do it all again. Entrepreneurs are a special breed.

You should know! If you're reading this book, then you're probably one of them.

One thing that can prevent your day job employer from selling their business is a rogue employee who claims ownership of the business. Consider how they'd feel receiving an email like this:

"Hey Boss, you know that widget that everyone likes so much which is the whole reason you're able to sell your business for millions of dollars? I designed that thing. It's mine. If you sell this business and don't pay me for it, I'm going to sue you."

A rogue employee threatening litigation is a very fast way to sink an acquisition deal. The PIIA you signed prevents you from claiming any ownership whatsoever for the work you did while employed for the company. It also goes further than that and says *anything* you worked on during your employment belongs to the company.

Anything? Really? What about your side projects?

Don't worry: there's a section in the PIIA that allows you to explicitly exclude something you worked on outside of your employment.

So long as you didn't use company property or company information in building your side project, you're clear. Just describe your project, play by the rules above, and you're fine.

There's more to the PIIA than assignment of rights, though. Buddy Arnheim, counsel to many startups and a partner at Perkins Coie, says there are three elements to the PIIA:

1. Intellectual property assignment;
2. Confidentiality agreement; and
3. Non-solicitation

Let's briefly discuss each of these elements.

Intellectual property (IP) assignment

This is the critical piece and the one that causes the most headaches for both employers and employees when they start side businesses. Whatever you work on, invent, produce, or create while an employee at someone else's business belongs to them. Full stop, end of story. If you use something you made at work for your side business and your employer challenges you, you'll probably lose. The law is against you in this case.

Buddy suggests, "If you're running a side project then you have to do it without any contamination of your employers resources. You shouldn't do it during working hours. Don't use your company-issued laptop or phone. Keep them as separate as possible. Don't even have email correspondence or other data going through your company office network."

Follow the rules above and you should be fine. The hard thing is to stick to it, don't cut corners, and do it 100% of the time. The one time you back down and tell yourself, "It's okay, I'll send this one email from my work computer or take this one call using the office phone in the conference room," is the one time that will get you. And then it won't matter that you followed the rules the other 99% of the time.

Another thing to consider if you own both of your businesses is how the intellectual property and source code rely on each other. Andrej, head of product at the AI studio I mentioned earlier, is running several companies, and one of them is planning to share parts of its source code publicly. The other will not. There are very specific rules about this practice of "open sourcing" a project and he is consciously keeping the IP completely separate even though the studio runs both companies.

Confidentiality agreement

Also known as a non-disclosure agreement (NDA), this part of the PIIA assumes you will learn trade secrets, intellectual property, and knowledge and techniques while employed at your day job. You have to keep these to yourself and not share them with other companies.

So if your side project is a contracting job with another company, you can't share what you know from your day job. Some employers go so far as to restrict side projects and contracting engagements simply because they recognize how difficult it can be to keep this firewall up. So rather than litigate it, they just outright restrict it.

In summary, not only can you not use IP that you created for your employer outside of work, you also can't use IP that other people created or that you learned while at work.

Non-solicitation agreement

This agreement typically states that if you leave your job you won't attempt to hire your former colleagues for a period of twelve months. If you leave and go full-time onto your side project, you won't be able to explicitly recruit others to join you. They may leave and work with you on their own volition, but it better be very clear that you didn't influence their departure.

When the tables turn

If any of this sounds harsh, put yourself in your employer's shoes. Or better yet, actually go out and start that business. If you hire anyone else, part-time or full-time, you will rest easier if you have them sign a PIIA for you. It's prudent and most contractors or employees won't object to the terms. If you ever sell your business you'll be rewarded for having the foresight to get these documents signed.

A quick plug for investing in real estate

The same proportion of parallel entrepreneurs I interviewed who ran SaaS companies also owned income-generating real estate.

Real estate is an evergreen investment. Yes, there are downturns, but it's a very safe bet that in the long run you will make good money. If you accumulate a lot of cash, property is a great place to park it.

And more importantly, unless you currently work in a real estate company, there will be no conflicts. You can safely run your own real estate holding company at nights and on weekends and keep your day job. If you have to respond to the one-off emergency call from a tenant (or better yet, a management company you pay to run your properties and support your tenants), then take it outside the office.

Income properties are a fine and potentially very lucrative way to earn income outside of your job and not have to worry about PIIAs, CODs, or getting in any sort of trouble with your boss or their lawyers.

JACK DORSEY
Co-founder of Twitter and Square

On October 4, 2015, Jack Dorsey was named Twitter's permanent CEO. Ten days later, Square was listed on the New York Stock Exchange. He was CEO of that company too.

If that's not parallel entrepreneurship then I don't know what is.

Twitter itself was born from a parallel track within Odeo, a once-popular podcasting service. Dorsey approached the founders with his idea for a status updating service that would fit within the constraints of the SMS text messaging system.

In March 2006, after several iterations on their product, Jack Dorsey posted the first-ever tweet: "just setting up my twttr." He became Twitter's first CEO and over the next ten years he would be its chairman, interim CEO, and once again its permanent CEO.

Dorsey originally lost his CEO position for leaving work early to do yoga and explore fashion design. So in May 2010, while he was chairman of Twitter, Dorsey launched Square with a co-founder. Square allowed shop owners to accept debit and credit card payments by swiping cards on a device attached to a smartphone.

In July 2015, Dorsey was promoted from chairman to interim CEO of Twitter and he continues to serve both Twitter and Square as CEO.

Jack Dorsey:
Twitter // Square

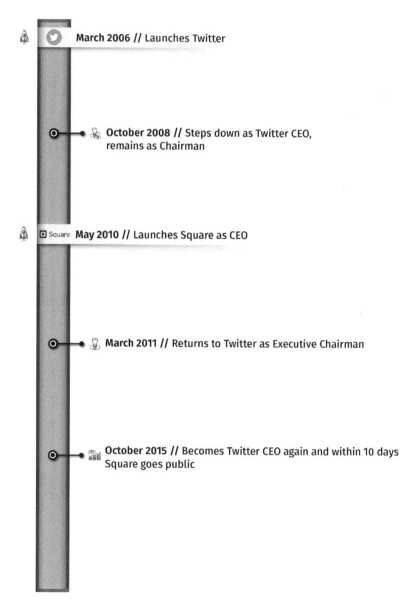

March 2006 // Launches Twitter

October 2008 // Steps down as Twitter CEO, remains as Chairman

Square **May 2010 //** Launches Square as CEO

March 2011 // Returns to Twitter as Executive Chairman

October 2015 // Becomes Twitter CEO again and within 10 days Square goes public

5

When to Quit

TOOFR IS NOW MY DAY job. It's my regular, low-risk salary and I'm continuing to build other businesses on the side.

My side businesses include a customer email tracker, an employee satisfaction surveyor, and a customer job change tracker. After several months of these web applications being live, however, only one of them has customers.

I will give these businesses a few more months of marketing support and then I will shut down the ones that aren't working. If a business is going to work, you should know within the first six months. You should be able to get people to use it regularly, which then gets people talking, which then generates inbound leads.

Here are three conditions for when you should quit your side business and start a different one.

When it drains rather than energizes you

If it's hard to muster the energy to work on it then you should probably stop, take a breather, and consider starting again on something else.

If your side business doesn't make you excited then you will have to be *extremely* lucky for it to work. Side projects that don't have your full creativity and enthusiasm are doomed to fail. It's as simple as that.

You, your family, and your friends are all better off if you spend that time watching TV, reading a book, or doing something else that makes you happy. Chances are far greater you'll find the right business to work on when you're happy than when you're stressed.

That's a universal truth in entrepreneurship.

When the market responds poorly

Most businesses fail. You'll hear this again and again, from MBAs, entrepreneurs, and the institutions who finance them, because it's true. Starting a business is hard and it usually doesn't work out.

This is all the more reason to start multiple businesses. The more you create, the better your odds are of finding success.

It's not just my advice. Jonathan Siegel says so too. Here's what he told me about parallel entrepreneurship and failure:

"Persistence helps you meet objectives, but I don't believe you can just persist through making a great company. Failure can take a long time. Success can happen very quickly. I always want to fail fast. Running more than one thing simultaneously reduces your amount of persistence on any one thing but gives you more tickets to find success."

It's worth noting that Jonathan runs a private equity fund with dozens of employees who operate a half dozen businesses. He is a pilot, owner of a chain of Irish pub restaurants, and a husband and father of eight. He has offices in Las Vegas, San Francisco, and Tokyo. We can't all be like Jonathan Siegel, but we can follow his advice about when to quit.

Let's say you're completely jazzed about this project. You tell everyone you know about it. You've built landing pages using Instapage or Unbounce and ran Google Ads to drive traffic to them and see how people respond.

And then…crickets. No one's clicking, signing up, or pressuring you to launch. Or maybe you were able to build the service yourself and even then, with a fully functioning application, the market says no.

It hurts. You don't want to give up, but even after iterating on taglines, pricing, and finding some clever ways to reach your target audience online, there are still no takers. When that happens you know at least one of these things is true:

- Your product is not differentiated enough; there are too many other players making too much noise for you to be heard.

- Your product isn't needed. Maybe it's a vitamin and not medicine, or maybe it's just a plain bad idea.

- You're wrong about who the customer is. Maybe your target customer isn't willing to pay, is hard to find online, or there actually aren't very many of them.

All of these cases are deadly. It's best to figure it out soon and take action. Six months is a good timeframe, given that you're only thinking about this right now on nights and weekends.

When the cost is too high

There are two kinds of costs to consider.

The first is tangible. It's the hard money cost of paying for servers, marketing, development, and sometimes data. Most of the time all of this is pretty cheap. You can get a year's worth of all of it for less than you might spend on an overseas vacation.

The other cost is much harder to pin down. It's the opportunity cost of *not* doing something else. Let me explain.

When you're in the throes of launching and running your side business, you don't have time for much else. You can't also be an overachiever at work, the first in and last to leave, even impressing your boss by showing up on the weekends. You need to spend those hours on your side business.

Because you will not be able to give it your all, you may lose out on rewards from your day job. Having a side business will keep you off the path to promotions because your nights and weekends will be spent on your side job instead of on projects at your current job. Be honest if your goal is to be promoted in your current position.

I still believe you should scrape together what little time you have left to become a parallel entrepreneur, even if it's just keeping a journal with notes and ideas. Accumulate those thoughts while you shoot for those promotions and bonuses.

If you prepare, you'll build your side business faster when the timing is better.

I think back on the time at Scripted when I was on-site during the day and building Toofr at home at night. I knew that I could have spent that time putting more effort into Scripted. But I also was aware that it wouldn't have mattered. I wasn't going to not get married, not have children, not have any sort of other life so I could work more.

I knew back then that it was about working smarter, not working longer hours. It was running a marathon, not a sprint. Toofr gave me energy and fresh ideas and actually made me more excited about going to work at Scripted.

When Not to Quit

— or —

How I Made a 5,000% Return on a Fancy Two-Day Vacation

IN LATE 2013, I WAS facing a bit of a crisis. I had just launched Toofr a few months earlier and it was failing.

Earlier that year, I found a way to automate email guessing using a public but hidden data source provided by a large social network. It worked amazingly well. It was fast, the data was terrific, and best of all, it was free.

But there was a catch. It was free because it wasn't supposed to be used for guessing emails.

Unfortunately, I wasn't alone in leveraging this harmless little hack. On November 23, 2013, another programmer wrote about it. About a week later, the source was effectively shut off and Toofr's primary data stream was gone.

My customers complained about poor data quality and many of them had been referred by my friends in the sales community.

These friends caught wind of the problems and kept pinging me, asking what was going on. My delay in fixing the problem was making them look bad.

I was working full-time on Scripted so I stayed up late and worked all of the following weekend trying to get the source to work again. In the meantime, I fell back to my pattern database but it was early and the data wasn't great yet. As December 2013 progressed, I felt increasingly guilty for continuing to charge my customers the same rates for an inferior product. They knew it too. The cancellations were piling up.

My wife and I planned to visit her family that December and take a two-day vacation at a nice resort south of Los Angeles. It was our third "personal retreat" where we'd go together to a fancy resort but maintain completely independent schedules. We might overlap for meals and drinks, but that's it. I would be free to work and stay up as late as I wanted, geeking out and tackling these Toofr problems. Likewise she could read, lie by the pool, and do her own projects. The idea was to give each other the creative freedom to do anything!

This retreat timing was perfect because I had a feeling that if I could just focus on the data source problem for 36 hours straight then I'd find a solution. I tried and failed to do it in the four-hour increments I was piecing together, so I used Scripted's winter shutdown to visit family and resolve my growing Toofr headache.

I remember sitting in the large, beautiful veranda overlooking the ocean and giving myself an ultimatum. If I couldn't get Toofr back on track and feel proud of my product, then I'd fold it up and dissolve the company. I'd have to do it before the year was up so I could save the additional $800 California LLC tax filing fee. I had these two days and then another two weeks to make the final decision.

With that singular focus in mind, I got to work.

My first plan of attack, admittedly, was to find a way back into the original data source. I tried all my tricks and made some progress but I couldn't get it to scale. I tossed out that approach.

The next morning I began to research other companies that provided this data for a fee. I looked at all of them, read their documentation and pricing, and extrapolated what their cost would be and what I might charge my customers. I was worried, again, that my particular use case might be against their terms of use. Ignorance is bliss, I figured, and didn't look to find out. I figured my volume would be too low to matter anyway.

I found a couple of good candidates and signed up for them, put down my credit card, and deployed my code on my last night of the retreat. I slept nervously that night, wondering if Toofr would still be functioning the next morning.

For the most part, it worked. Toofr was stable and my customers were happy again. I felt better about continuing to charge them. Toofr had new life. The end of December came and went and I decided not to shut it down.

Over the following months, I continued to fret about Toofr being blocked by either or both of the data vendors. I was paying for the data, and everything was above board, but if they looked at the way I was using it and disapproved, I might lose access. It didn't keep me up at night or distract from Scripted, but the concern was always there.

Toofr continued to grow in 2013 and broke $50,000 in 2014.

The year 2015 was huge as Toofr nearly tripled in revenue. I credit that growth to a lot of power users speaking up and boosting word of mouth referrals. It slowed down the following year, 2016, but still grew a respectable 35 percent.

I was spending several thousand dollars each month on data throughout 2015 and 2016, and as I'd feared, my account eventually did get flagged. My vendors asked to speak to me and I scheduled a call and confessed.

Instead of shutting me down, though, they increased my fees and made me sign annual licenses. Relieved to not face yet another data crisis, I obliged. It's been nice and steady and stable ever since.

To sum it up, in its first year Toofr made less than $3,000. When I spent that weekend at the St. Regis working to fix it, that's all I knew. Toofr made some money, and it might make a lot more, but it also might make nothing. Going into that weekend, Toofr really wasn't working. I had unhappy customers and a lot of unwanted stress.

If I shut it down that month, I'd save $800 in tax filing fees the following year. That's a lot of money, so it was tempting to just kill it.

As it turned out, killing it would have been a very, very costly mistake. Toofr's lifetime revenue now is over $550,000. Those two nights at the St. Regis, plus meals and drinks, were about $1,100. That's a 5,000% return on investment!

I've been taking personal retreats each December ever since and it goes to show that yes, sometimes your side project is a pain in the you-know-what. It's bound to happen, but you can still deal with it without impacting your day job.

TACTICS

*"Man, I don't even know how to **spell** 'entrepreneur'."*

—a friend of mine, Harvard Business School graduate,
and self-described "wantrepreneur."

*"The only thing more overrated than natural childbirth
is the joy of owning your own business."*

—a quote on the wall at the Creekside Cafe in Sonoma, CA

THERE'S NO SINGLE WAY TO begin building your company. One day, it just starts.

It might have been a conversation over beers, an article you read that sparked an idea, or a lingering notion in the back of your mind that finally manifests itself as a napkin sketch on an airplane.

Whatever that starting point is, at some point, you just *start*.

The tactics I've compiled and am sharing here are the culmination of a decade of starting things. I didn't form my first company until after college, but I've been starting things up since high school. After dozens of conversations with friends trying to "get into startups," and dozens more with successful entrepreneurs to research this book, I have compiled a very tactical how-to guide for the modern entrepreneur.

The underpinning thesis is that if you're serious about succeeding and changing your life, then you can and should have at least two irons in the fire. You can and should have two ways to make a living and do what you love.

These tactics show you how to do it with an online subscription-based software business.

Reminder: You Only Need 100 Customers

YOU DON'T NEED TO TAKE a company or two public in order to be a successful parallel entrepreneur. You only need 100 customers paying you an average of $100 per month.

That's it!

And by the way, those 100 customers could be all for the same business, or they could be spread across two or three businesses. Get there by any means necessary and you'll have reached the promised land.

This is the beauty of software-as-a-service (SaaS) businesses. Jonathan Siegel, the parallel entrepreneur and founder of Xenon Ventures I introduced earlier, loves SaaS business.

"I am bullish on SaaS because of the high customer value and low friction for building and maintaining the customer relationship," he told me.

Jonathan believes there's low friction because there is human factor error. Billing someone's credit card again and again is relatively new. Before this you needed a sales person to close and manage a high value relationship. Now you can do that with a credit card, which doesn't feel like money to the customer.

This recurring credit card billing phenomenon leads to some great business opportunities.

A hundred customers paying $100 per month adds up to $120,000 per year of revenue. Since we're building software, you'll have about 85% gross margins, so your gross profit could be at least $100,000.

Your operating expenses are business-related assets and advertising activities, some of which will neatly cross over into your personal life (tax write-off for your home office, for example). Let's say those expenses cost another $30,000 per year, so your "in-the-bank" net profit is $70,000.

That's the big picture. That's what you're shooting for.

It's a business that makes enough income for you to pay rent, even if you live in San Francisco or New York. If your home base is anywhere else, then you're living like self-made royalty.

You may still need dual income to save for a house and take nice vacations, but what you've done with your $120,000 business is bought yourself time and flexibility. You might even keep your day job. Or you'll start building a second $120,000 business because your first one pretty much runs itself.

This is when you feel rich, free, independent, and on top of the world. Even if you don't have a million dollars in the bank, you'll feel like you do, and your lifestyle won't be that much different than the millionaire class. Except you'll probably work a lot less, spend more time with your family, and sleep better.

That's what it means to be a parallel entrepreneur. You don't wait until your plate is empty before you start another business. You just spin another one up and see if it grows as nicely as your first one.

It's "and"—not "or"—when you're clearing $10,000 month with a SaaS business that runs itself. You can pretty much do anything you want.

Here are a few points about how to make this work. We'll dive into these in more detail throughout this part of the book:

- **Sell to businesses**. Businesses don't mind spending $100 per month on a service that delivers value. It's likely you'll fly right under the radar during those inevitable months when they barely log into your product. Businesses these days are conditioned to accept monthly software fees. Take advantage of it!

- **Pick a problem that's never really solved**. The beautiful thing about sales leads is you never stop needing them. That's why Toofr is a great little business. When it works (it finds good emails and generates good leads) it makes the users (sales reps and recruiters) want more. So the monthly nature of the billing actually makes sense!

- **Automate as much as you can**. If you're going to actually enjoy running a small business yourself or keep your team lean enough so you're able to keep a ratio of $100K in profit per employee, then you need to automate. A lot. Often that means signing up for other people's software products. I love supporting other parallel entrepreneurs.

- **Focus on one problem per business**. If you try to do too much at one time, you'll burn cash without increasing your company's value. Your investors will lose steam and you won't have the traction you need to be competitive. Instead, focus on doing one thing that adds value. Diane Baxter, a CFO at Kranz & Associates sums it up nicely, "If you want to do parallel entrepreneurship, then have multiple singularly-focused business with different boards and different investors."

It will take some time to get there on a bootstrapped shoe-string budget, but you'll get those 100 customers eventually. Just stick to the game plan and stay tuned in to your market.

Business Structure

You don't need a partner

DON'T START WITH THE ASSUMPTION that you need a partner. That's a mistake that I see far too often. Give yourself more credit than that.

You're an entrepreneur, right? Figure it out yourself!

I interviewed fifteen successful parallel entrepreneurs for this book and focused a lot on their skill sets. There are at least a dozen common tasks that employees at software companies have to do, everything from coding to running marketing campaigns and analyzing finances. You might be surprised that only half of the entrepreneurs I spoke to could write their own software.

If you want to put yourself among the ranks of parallel entrepreneurs living the high life with a skill set that you can deploy anywhere, then you should do as much as possible yourself. Not everyone is going to be an engineer. No problem! You can learn to do everything else and delegate the rest.

Max Altschuler is great at outsourcing. "In most cases, I find it best to leverage my expertise, experience, network, and money to work for me, instead of having to do too much heavy lifting. My time is worth more than it would cost someone more proficient to do it for me."

Max is the sole founder of Sales Hacker and outsourced all his technical development. This is not unusual. Jonathan Siegel told me of the many managers he's hired and worked with, he sees no correlation between success and how technical the manager is. This is from a guy with three degrees in computer science!

The most important benefit of not having a partner is the lower bar to profitability and freedom.

I started this section telling you that you only need 100 customers to be successful. Well, that's only true if you do this yourself. If you have a partner then you need 200 customers. If you have three partners, then you need 300 customers. You see how this math works?

If it takes two years to get 100 customers, then it might take another year to get a second 100 customers. You've delayed your freedom by a year. And for what? Nine times out of ten it's completely unnecessary.

A far better approach is to get those 100 customers on your own. Then you're free.

And now that you're free, you can *choose* to either continue as a solopreneur or bring on a partner. You can start that partner part-time or use some of your savings to go in the red so long as you're certain that future growth will put you back in the black. Or you can take out a small business loan.

The best news is this: you can still own 100% of your business after you bring on this partner. In fact, this partner is really just your first employee, but you can bestow upon them a "partner" status and grant them equity if it's warranted.

Or not. You're the boss. You have the keys. It's totally up to you.

The standard blueprint for solopreneur success is to be a good product manager and an excellent marketer. Tactically, you should focus on the marketing. No one is in a better position to compel the market to try and buy a new product than the founder.

You can outsource software development. You can even outsource product management so long as you have a clear vision of the final product, sketches or mockups, and a very specific list of features for your MVP.

You should not outsource your marketing. Certainly not all of it. You can hire talented freelancers on websites like Upwork to help with design, paid advertising, and content creation, but whether you like it or not, as the sole founder of the company, you are the chief marketing officer.

If you don't like it, or if the hat simply doesn't fit, then you should stop your entrepreneurial journey right here or find a business partner who loves marketing with the same fervor that you love building or managing product.

Let's look more closely at that option.

If you do have a partner, then product and marketing should be evenly split

Initially, your business structure and your team structure should look like this.

Co-founder A: Runs marketing (and usually is the CEO)

Co-founder B: Builds product (and usually is the CTO)

To make the distinction clearer, here are the two critical pathways to launching a product: marketing and product development.

Critical marketing launch activities	Critical product launch activities
Company name, logo, and tagline	MVP definition and timeline
Homepage design and copy	Feature development
SEO and digital marketing	Database schema development
Pricing and funnel optimization	Bug and feature tracking

The allure of having a partner is strong. You may decide, as I have, to partner with people who have a unique ability to succeed at marketing activities. This is why I chose to have a partner for Inlistio and I've recently begun another business with a different partner.

In both cases, my partners help on the marketing side so I can focus on product. With many parallel businesses running, I can't do it all anymore. Having business partners helps me scale.

I'm good enough at building products to produce a "minimum viable product" (MVP) for any idea. As a result, I don't need engineering help. That part is easy and enjoyable for me. The hard part, and what I don't like as much, is launching and getting the first customers to use my product. I get what might be called "marketing block" and clam up, look away, and go back into the code.

A good partner for me is someone who loves to promote products and has direct access to a network of potential customers.

Here's a truth that most entrepreneurs learn the hard way, myself included: Good products don't sell themselves.

It's true. You can spend all of your time or somebody else's time refining every last pixel, squashing every bug, and releasing every possible feature for your ideal customer. Without marketing, though, your project is toast. It doesn't matter how good or how beautiful it is.

It took me ten years to say this but here it is: marketing is everything.

So I don't partner for the sake of partnering. I'm very selective about whom I work with now, especially if the partnership involves a separate entity that we share ownership of.

Under no conditions should you have a third co-founder. If you go that route then you are adding 50% more friction to your decision-making process, extending launch times, and ultimately delaying your ability to support yourself by at least a year.

The decisions you make about business structure and who you start your business with are fundamentally critical decisions. You should not take any of them lightly. If it blows up in your face, a bad move here can and will doom your business. Business partners don't go away easily. When they do, it leaves a permanent scar.

Michael Lovitch, co-founder of the prestigious Babybathwater Institute and a supplements e-commerce company, says, "You always need to build better teams." I completely agree, and in that quest for perfection you may need to let go of employees.

It's a lot more difficult to let go of business partners. You can avoid that trap by hiring your top talent instead of partnering with them.

Only have a partner if it's absolutely necessary and you're completely sure that there's no other way to do it.

Structure your business as a LLC

Toofr is a LLC (limited liability corporation). Scripted was a C-corporation. I've done it both ways, and I can tell you something with great certainty: LLCs are much better.

C-corporations allow you to create a large operation, grant options to future employees, issue stock to investors, build a board of directors, and take your company public. This is overkill. You don't need it when you first start your company, but everybody wants to form C-corporations. Don't follow the hype!

You absolutely should create a separate business entity, though. It's cleaner for tax purposes, demonstrates legitimacy to your customers, and ultimately protects you from lawsuits that might impact you personally.

Also if you decide to sell your business it's a clean break from you personally. Your business interests are all tied together under the business structure. The legal documents are easy to understand and the transaction fees will be minimized.

Here's a breakdown of the differences between each type of business structure.

	LLC	S-Corporation	C-Corporation
Ownership	"Members"	"Shareholders"	"Shareholders"
Salary	1099	W2	W2
Options	No	Yes	Yes
Stock	No	Yes	Yes
Pass-through income	Yes	Yes	No
Annual taxes	Easy	Easy	Hard
Annual reporting	Simple	Moderate	Complex

I prefer LLCs because they give all of the same legal benefits as a C- or S-corporation without the reporting requirements.

When it comes to taxes, your single-member LLC is filed along with your personal income taxes. It's called a pass-through entity because the profit or loss from your LLC is presented on the IRS Schedule K form with your personal taxes.

You don't need to file anything separately for your business. This is a huge benefit for solopreneurs. Any tax accountant can do this for you for cheap or, if you want, you can do it yourself using TurboTax.

It's all documented and been done literally a million times by thousands of entrepreneurs just like you. When I file my Toofr LLC taxes, I just send my tax accountant my annual income statement. She'll ask me a few clarifying questions about it and that's it. She only needs one piece of information from me. I pay about $300 per year to prepare and file my personal and business taxes.

All of my other businesses fall under Toofr LLC. The income and expenses for Inlistio, eNPS, Thinbox, and everything else go under Toofr LLC and are filed together. I don't have a separate LLC for each internet business because it doesn't matter. There's no benefit to doing that.

I'll explain in the next section how I account for them separately, but for legal and tax purposes, it's actually just a single business. I can only think of one very good reason to break them into separate entities: an acquisition. Until then, they're all under a single legal umbrella.

Here's a quick breakdown of the costs to form and operate a LLC in California. Exact costs will vary from state-to-state but they'll all be roughly the same.

Formation
- *$20 filing fee. It's a single form you can fill out yourself or use any number of online services.*
- *$800 initial minimum tax. Send a check and simple paperwork to the Secretary of State.*

Operation
- *$800/year minimum tax due to the State Franchise Board.*
- *$100/year in additional accounting overhead and/or TurboTax fees.*

Eventually these costs won't matter. They'll be a drop in the bucket. But when you're starting out, dropping a minimum of $1,000 per year just on legal and taxes feels excessive. Funnel that frustration into marketing and developing your business. It will sting less the second year, and by the third year you won't even think about it.

You should create the LLC no earlier than when you start spending money to market and build your business and no later than when your customers start paying you. You can do everything as a sole proprietor without a federal employee ID number (EIN) but for protection and organization, I recommend forming an LLC.

Another important characteristic of the LLC is it doesn't have shareholders. The owners of a LLC are called "members" and each member has a specific percentage ownership of the LLC. If you're a single founder, you can file in your state as single-member LLC which of course implies that you're the owner and have 100% of the membership.

If despite all my warnings and explanations above you decide you need to have a partner, then you and your partner will have to decide how to split up the membership.

It's easy to split it right down the middle with each partner getting 50% of the LLC. Be wary of that arrangement.

If anything should go astray, you will not have control of your business. If it's your idea, you got started first, and you're putting in more of your own time or money to launch the business, then you should get at least 51 percent. Your partner should be okay with that.

It may feel adversarial at first, but if it's the true, honest depiction of the reality of how your business started, then a good partner will understand. I'm not a small business attorney and won't go into what that 51% gets you in the case of a conflict, but it will make it far easier to resolve disputes when you have the majority stake. It's worth the awkwardness upfront to have that assurance.

The other implication is you won't be able to give your future employees stock or options. I've decided that I'm okay with this. Employees shouldn't count on stock in a small business to be of any value, and you shouldn't feel pressured to offer employees liquidity. Your goal here is set yourself up for financial freedom. Instead of giving them stock, give employees a great place to work, chances to grow and learn, and a nice paycheck.

But we're getting ahead of ourselves. By the time you can afford to hire full-time staff, you'll already have a successful business on your hands. You can do whatever you want, including converting your LLC into a C-corporation and taking your company public.

Cross that bridge when you get there. Two-thirds of the parallel entrepreneurs I interviewed agree: Start your business as a limited liability corporation.

Open a separate business checking account as soon as you start spending money

Another reason to form your legal business entity is you'll need it to open a business checking account at your local bank.

Until then, since you may incur costs before you officially

form your business, I recommend opening a second personal checking account. You or your accountant will be glad you did. It'll keep your financial data clean and easy to follow. This will pay off down the road, even if you decide not to form your legal entity for a year or more.

I can't overstate how important it is to keep clean books. Simple hygiene like this pays dividends later on. When you lose track of your finances you lose track of your business. You can't operate as a solopreneur if you don't know where your cash is going, how much your marketing and development costs each month, and how deep of a hole you're digging before paying customers start to bail you out.

A dedicated checking account, whether personal or business, is a must-have when you start your business. By the time you're earning income, you can make a new business checking account, transfer the balance to it, and close your second checking account. Your accounting software will tie the accounting histories together.

The main difference between personal and business checking is your business account will have your business name, which looks more professional for accepting checks and wires, and typically will include features that allow you to give access to employees and accountants. So while it's preferred to have a business account, you can get by with a personal one. You just need to keep your business income and expenses separate from your personal life.

When you start running multiple businesses in parallel, I've found that you can funnel the income and expenses into the same business checking account so long as it's easy to separate them in your accounting software. I'll dive into this tactic more in the next section, but suffice to say for now, you can run multiple businesses on a single checking account. Create a new checking account for your second or third businesses only when the bookkeeping process requires it.

Summary

Simplicity pays. My recommendations here are the simplest way to structure your business. A single founder (you) doing both marketing and product activities provides the lowest hurdle to financial freedom. It also allows you to create the simplest form of a limited liability corporation, the single-member LLC.

Start with the assumption that this is the best route. Challenge yourself every time you think you need a partner. If you absolutely need a partner now and can't wait a year or even six months when it will be much easier to justify having a majority of the LLC membership, then make every effort keep for yourself at least 51 percent.

Finally, there's no excuse to mix your business and personal funds. Any bank will grant you a second personal checking account. If you haven't created your LLC by the time you're starting to spend money on your business, funnel all expenses (and eventually income) through that second personal account. When the income comes, immediately create the LLC and a business checking account and then transfer the balance to it and close the second personal account. You can tie the histories together with your accounting software.

These steps are critical to laying a foundation of clean ownership, expectations, and financial data.

Do not underestimate the importance of being very diligent at this stage of your business!

Ideation

WE ALL FACE CHALLENGES IN our daily life. A viable business is one that addresses a challenge that a lot of people face. People pay for things that make their lives or their jobs easier. It's as simple as that.

Remember, businesses will buy faster and pay more for products than consumers will. It's a lot easier to get 100 customers (threshold for making a living on a B2B company) than 10 million viewers (threshold for making a living on a B2C app or website).

The average revenue per user (ARPU) of a B2B software customer should be at least $100 per month. Remember the example earlier? 100 customers paying $100 per month is $120,000 of revenue and $102,000 of profit.

What happens if your ARPU drops to $10 per month? Now you need 1,000 customers, not 100. That's a ten-fold increase in your marketing needs, which also means more time for you to struggle, second-guess, and perhaps give up.

It gets worse. Netflix hesitated to ask people to pay $10 per month and took years to do it, so you'll probably struggle too.

Let's say your typical B2C customer pays $5 per month. Now you need 2,000 customers to get $100,000 per year in profit. That's a 20-fold increase in costly customer acquisition, and besides that, we don't want to deal with 2,000 customers. Think of all the support emails you'll get!

This is assuming you can get people to pay. Most B2C ideas make referral or advertiser revenue. Then the numbers get even more daunting. I hear from my B2C-oriented friends that having one million monthly active viewers gets you an investor meeting. Having 10 million monthly actives gets you a lifestyle business.

That's too much work for me. Let's go the easier route and sell to businesses.

Idea Discovery

You need to address a pain point that people face in their jobs. The possibilities are endless! You just have to listen to your colleagues, conversations on Twitter, or sessions at conferences. If you're struggling to get ideas, then talk to your friends. Here are some questions you can ask:

- What's the worst part of your workday?
- What do you like least about your job?
- What could you do a lot faster if you just had the right tool?
- What task do you wish you could hand off to someone else?

People are expensive. At a typical small company, salaries are at least 80% of their operating expenses. There's a reason why your friend can't just hand off her least favorite tasks to a new hire. Her boss won't allow it!

But if you could not only take that pain point but also do it better for only $100 a month, would her boss care? Doubt it. She'll just hand you the company credit card.

That's the kind of problem you need to solve and the kind of customer you need to solve it for. Let me elaborate.

There are many kinds of B2B customers.

First, there are users of the product who want to use it because it makes their jobs easier.

Then there are the managers who may not care about the features of your product, so long as it improves their bottom line by reducing costs or making their direct reports more productive.

Finally, there are the business owners who are looking down the field to anticipate market or competitor moves.

The customers you want are the *users* of the product. They give you good feedback, they are easy to identify and meet (for most people, they are their peers), and they can usually get a simple verbal approval on a $100 per month spend. Mostly importantly, there are a lot of them. As in millions.

Why not sell to managers and business owners?

Managers and owners are tricky to sell to. They are hard to get a hold of, and they want to talk the language of value, not features. Early on, you probably won't know the value of what you're building. You won't have case studies with managers saying things like, "Acme Business Software has made my employees 10% more productive each month, saving me $500,000 per year." That's what a manager wants to hear, and they'll also expect to sign an annual contract and get the customer support that comes with it. You don't want to deal with this. Perhaps later on it's okay to explore it, but certainly not when you first start.

Don't get tempted by large contracts with big numbers. Prove out your concept first with a group of lower-paying monthly customers. The big guys will always be there, and if you want to sell up market, you'll be able to charge more if you wait and polish off the bugs first.

To reiterate, your idea should address a pain point that a large number of people feel at work. Choose a market that you're familiar with. For example, if you've worked in sales, then think about the most annoying part of a sales rep's job. That's what I did when I built Toofr, and it paid off.

Your idea should solve a clear pain that you've felt personally or people around you feel.

The other critical characteristic of a great B2B business idea is that it should never fully satisfy the customer. Their cup should never be full. They should always need more of your product.

Example: The SEO market has no finish line

A good example of a business category that will never fully satisfy its customers is the search engine optimization (SEO)
market. Marketers who work to improve SEO are never done.
They will never arrive at work, fire up their screens, and say,
"Huzzah! I made it. My SEO is perfect and I can go home early."

No, the nature of online marketing is the tides are ever-shift-
ing, the challenges ever-increasing, and the whims of Google
ever-changing. Even when you're well positioned in organic
search results, you need software to maintain that position, to
watch the moves of your competition, and stay one step ahead.

So if you're a data or software provider in the SEO market
and provide an excellent product, then your customers will never
leave you because they think your job is done. It's not like software development where there's a clearly defined finish line. In
SEO, you need a set of software tools to constantly monitor the
data and adjust your strategies.

The cup is never full. There's no finish line. It's an ongoing
need that will never go away.

This is a great business to be in. But before you put this book
down and dash off to build your SEO product, know that we're
not alone with this insight. Markets with needs like this are very
competitive. The SEO software and data provision market is
saturated.

Fortunately there are others. In markets like this the ten-
dency is for demand to expand. You can still carve out your own
little niche within the market and get your 100 customers.

I simply suggest that you ask this question about the problem you're solving: Is there ever a finish line? If not, that's a very good thing. All else being equal, I'd choose that idea over any others.

Use this Idea Discovery Template to choose which ideas to test

Before going into the testing phase, I suggest you take a deep dive into five ideas. Talk to people, friends, family, colleagues, and ask these questions below. Write down the answers for all five. Pick the one or two ideas that you're most excited about and then start testing them in the next section.

To help determine which idea to go with, do this short exercise for five unique business ideas:

Text answers
- *Describe the idea:*
- *Describe who will buy it:*

Yes/no answers
- *Do you personally need this product?*
- *Can you visualize how the finished product will look and feel?*
- *Do you already have a logo or name for the business in mind?*
- *Do you know where to find these customers?*
- *Is there a finish line?*

Here's a quick note about this technique. I asked you to write down descriptions of your product and customers first so you subliminally start to feel the business form in your head. Then, I toggle to quick tactical and emotional questions. You need to be motivated, and the best way to gauge excitement is how quickly your creative brain kicks in.

If you can visualize the product already, then that's a very good sign. There's enough inherent difficulty in building a business no matter what. Some of it should be fun and easy. It should feel rewarding to build because you're solving a problem for yourself too. If you know where to find your customers and are confident they'll never stop needing a solution, you'll find a faster path to success.

Now add up one point for every "yes" answer. The one or two with the highest scores should move on to testing.

Idea Testing

Much has been written about how to efficiently test your idea. Tim Ferriss, Eric Ries, and many others offer great templates and examples. The basic tactic is simple: test your idea using online ads and landing pages before you start building it.

The risk of diving straight into building the application MVP is that you may have defined your MVP incorrectly. It may have the wrong features, the wrong pricing, or the wrong approach to the pain you're attempting to solve.

You won't know that your assumptions are off target until you put it in front of a lot of people. The point of idea testing is you don't need to actually build your tool in order to test demand. You can build a basic page that describes your solution, your pricing, and your features, and then ask people to submit their email addresses for updates.

Granted, there's a big leap between a prospect giving you their email address and making a credit card purchase. I am not confusing the two but I am suggesting that your success in attracting email addresses is a good and inexpensive indicator of success in attracting paying customers. It's much better to get that data upfront than to build the wrong thing and lose a lot of valuable time and money.

You might still be wondering why I suggest you do all of this testing if the whole point is to run multiple companies at once. Fair point!

I still stand by this diligence because you want to pick winners. Parallel entrepreneurship is about spinning up the right businesses so you can accumulate 100 customers across multiple businesses faster.

Including a dud in your online business portfolio will only prolong the process. Good idea testing minimizes that risk.

Landing page testing

A landing page is a single page with a single purpose. At this point in the process, the purpose is to capture email addresses from people interested in your future launch.

Your landing page should have the following three components:

- A brief tagline ("Quickly find anybody's email address!")
- A call to action ("Get early access! Join our newsletter!")
- Three or four key benefits ("Fast, easy, affordable")

All three items, the tagline, call to action (CTA,) and benefit list should be "above the fold." This old-fashioned newspaper term means no one should have to scroll down to see them.

Below the fold you can begin to experiment with additional information, like in-depth feature descriptions, testimonials, screenshots or screencasts, or your origin story. You can use tools like CrazyEgg to track scroll depth to see if people are seeing this content.

Finally, it's important to test multiple variations of a landing page. I recommend just two variants to start, and tools like Unbounce and Instapage make it very easy to do this. You will not need to do any programming or page hosting yourself, and they'll track the success of each variation (you'll tell Unbounce or Instapage, for example, that "success" is capturing an email address.)

Also, the landing page software you choose will likely include professional design templates that are easily customized so you don't need to start from a blank page. Choose the design you like the best and then change the colors, icons, and text, and you're ready to go!

These are the questions that your landing page experiment needs to answer:

- How should I describe the problem my product solves?
- Which benefit do my customers need most?
- Is this an urgent need or an opportunistic need?
- How much are my customers willing to pay for it?

Let's go through each question individually with some specific tactics to get to the heart of the question.

How should I describe the problem my product solves?

If you answered "yes" to the question on the Idea Discovery Survey about whether or not *you* need this tool, then start by writing the description to yourself as the customer. What description would entice you to buy? Write it down using as few words as possible.

If you're not personally in the ideal customer set, then try your hardest to put yourself there. You may need to do some more research to figure it out. Talk to you friends, find competitors on Google, and rephrase the solution in a way that makes sense to you.

For example, maybe you've heard that cannabis suppliers are having a really hard time creating labels for their products. You enjoy product marketing and design and want to build an online labeling software for the cannabis industry. You're not a cannabis seller so you can't speak to it directly as a potential customer, but it's not too difficult to imagine what they might want to hear.

Something like, "Quickly create compliant labeling for cannabis products." That would be the main description of your product. Short, snappy, nothing left for interpretation or extrapolation. You make labels for cannabis products and you sell to cannabis producers. If I'm one of them and feeling this pain, I would sign up for updates.

For testing, I recommend choosing wildly different taglines on your homepage. Emphasize a different benefit or reason to use your product. Call out the benefits rather than features. Rather than say, "Acme Widgets *does* X," say, "Acme Widgets *gives you* X."

In the above example, the benefit is that it's fast and compliant. A poor description would read, "Upload your cannabis products and get labels in return."

Which benefits do my customers need most?

By testing descriptions that emphasize one specific benefit, you can use the email submission conversion rates to tell how important that benefit is to your potential customers.

Another place to test benefits is below the tagline, where you might have text in a smaller font, usually bulleted, that dives further into the scope of your product.

For example:

- Select from five industry-standard templates.
- Expert legal review included.
- Fits products of all sizes.

Once you've identified the best description, you can run more experiments by keeping the description the same and completely changing the benefits bullets or altering the order.

Is this an urgent need or an opportunistic need?

A silent killer of your campaign is a lack of urgency among your prospects. This can be very difficult to see in advance and is demoralizing to a solo founder. You can gauge a sense of urgency by testing the language of your CTA.

For one version of the page, make it loud and clear that there's *scarcity*. Either say you're only going to invite the first 20 signups, or that you have 50 early bird coupons to offer, or you'll turn off the signup form at the end of the month.

Then run another version of the page that has a typical "Join Now" or "Learn More" CTA. See if there's a significant difference in conversion. If there's not, your customers may not have a burning need. You'll likely see longer and more complex sales cycles. The pain may not be as acute as you'd hoped.

This doesn't mean it's a bad business to go into. It just means you will need to reach a larger audience and build up more slowly using organic traffic rather than paid traffic. I'll describe these differences in the **Growing** chapter.

No difference between the urgent call to action approach and the standard call to action approach also means this business might be a good candidate for parallel entrepreneurship. But since it will take some time to get traction, put it up, nurture it, and slowly build the product, don't count on it for income any time soon.

If you do get a significant increase in conversion (the urgent call to action converted more people), then you have a hungry customer market and you should move ahead to pricing and building as quickly as possible.

A quick note about testing button colors: just stop.

Don't bother experimenting with button colors or dramatically different designs. We're testing the crux of your business idea here and it will not be made or broken by which font and color pallette you use. You can learn this the hard way, on your own, or you can heed my advice. I hope you choose the latter.

How much are my customers willing to pay for it?

This is the easiest experiment to do. It's cut and dry logistically and it should be the last experiment you run.

Once you've arrived at the best description and set of CTAs, you should keep those constant while you play with pricing.

My favorite approach is to come up with your ideal set of prices. Remember, 100 customers paying $100 each, right? The *average* customer needs to pay you $100, so if you have three plans, that $100 price should be in the middle.

The experiment you should run is whether or not to have a plan under $100. If you can get good conversion rates by displaying, say, a $100 per month and a $250 per month plan, then that's very good news. You might still have a $50 per month plan, but save it for an email newsletter promotion to high risk customers. You don't need to show it to everybody.

Far too often entrepreneurs underprice their products. The

more you charge, the less work you ultimately have to do. And the fact is, most online B2B businesses are *price inelastic*. This means that demand doesn't change much with pricing. Business owners usually don't feel a difference between a $50 per month product and a $150 per month product. They won't churn over pricing.

So if your market allows it, price high. Start high and adjust downward because it's often easier to lower prices than to raise them.

A quick primer on the statistics of landing page testing

You don't need to be a math whiz to figure out when a landing page variation is statistically significant. The landing page applications you'll use to run these will do that calculation for you. However, it's still important for you to understand what's going on and how to interpret the results.

The best landing page experiments test *only one change*. Consider a case where you have two landing pages that are completely identical except for the top tagline. When you run the two variations through your landing page software, you can attribute a significant conversion rate difference to the change in description. That's cut and dry.

But what if you throw another change in there? What if you included a pricing change along with the description change? Now you have two pages each with two variations, so to fully test this, you'd actually need to run four unique landing pages.

It might be easier to visualize it this way:

	Pricing A	**Pricing B**
Description A	**LP #1: DA, PA**	LP #2 DA, PB
Description B	LP #3: DB, PA	**LP #4: DB, PB**

There are four variations needed to test, but you're testing only LP #1 and LP #4! The landing page software will run whatever variations you give it. It doesn't know that you've changed multiple things on both pages. So if you get a better result with Landing Page #4, you won't know if it's because of Description B, Pricing B, or both. You need to run LP #1, #2, and #3 too.

If you add a third element, then it gets even harder. Instead of four variations, you'll have nine, and so on.

You might say, so what? I'll just run the four or nine variations. If you want to pay for that traffic, then sure, but traffic costs money. People aren't going to just stumble upon your landing page, and clicks from your Twitter or Facebook pages will have bias. As we'll read in the next section, you'll need to pay for ads to drive traffic to your landing pages.

The more variations you have, the more traffic you'll need, the longer it will take, and the more cash you'll have to pay to get the results.

It's better to have fewer variants, ideally one change per experiment. So I suggest you run them sequentially.

Create a landing page with your best guess on each of the above sections. You have to put a stick in the sand somewhere, and a landing page with no pricing at all may lead to buyer confusion. So put your best guess down and then change one thing at a time. Start with the description, move on to the benefits and CTA, and then finally to the price.

▶ CASE STUDY: Inlistio

1 month and 23 days. This is equal to 14.5% of a year.

That's how long it took to go from idea to first revenue in the bank for **Inlistio**, a company I launched in my quest for a parallel revenue stream alongside Toofr.

It's an important reminder of how long it can take to get your SaaS company launched and making revenue.

A friend and entrepreneur I admire, Max Altschuler, sent me an email describing his idea on July 16, 2017. He asked me, "Would you pay for a piece of software that tells you when a user or subscriber leaves the company, what company they go to, and what their new email address is?"

I told him I'd had a similar thought for one of my side projects and investigated it enough to discover some non-obvious ways to grab the data. "Wanna collaborate on that?" I asked.

"Yes. Yes I do," he replied.

A few days later, on July 21, I had a GitHub repository for my code, a Heroku account for hosting, and very basic Ruby on Rails application live and running. (I'll explain what each of these are later in the Building section.)

Almost exactly a month later, on August 22, I "launched" Inlistio on social media. It had actually been up and live for a couple of weeks, but this was the first time I said it loud and proud. We both posted about it on LinkedIn and Facebook.

I ultimately changed the pricing three times, and then finally on September 7, nearly two weeks after that announcement, I got our first customer. It took us just under two months to go from idea to first revenue and for the next few months it averaged only one new customer every month. It took five months to get the first $1,000 of monthly recurring revenue.

The lesson here is this: even if you're quick to launch, getting customers and traction still takes a while. Here's what I wrote on social media when we launched:

> Today I released https://www.inlistio.com to the world with my friend and fellow sales tech entrepreneur, Max Altschuler.
>
> From idea (when Max sent me an email describing the problem) to launch it took just under 5 weeks! Record time considering we're both occupied with other businesses.
>
> Inlistio alerts sales reps, business owners, and marketing leaders when their contacts switch jobs.
>
> Why does that matter?
>
> - Job changes cause accounts to cancel or downgrade.
> - Job changes also open up new business opportunities.
>
> How do you grow a business? Reduce churn and get new customers.
>
> Inlistio helps with both!

I like this post because it clearly states what Inlistio does (tracks job changes) and why it's valuable (reduces churn and increases customer acquisition).

Unfortunately, I got a lot of likes and registrations but no customers. Not a single one. I included 20 contacts for free, so anyone could kick the tires. I wanted to give some free data so I wouldn't have to give demos for everyone.

I launched with this pricing:

> Bottom tier: $199/mo for 200 contacts
> Middle tier: $499/mo for 1,000 contacts
> Top tier: $999/mo for 5,000 contacts

Since I had a business partner on this one and we were going to split profits, I wanted to have higher value customers. At the time I launched Inlistio, Toofr was making over $18,000 a month of profit. I was anxious to get Inlistio up there as quickly as possible.

Unfortunately, customers don't work that way. They don't care about your other businesses and how much money they're making. I waited a few days and lowered the prices:

> Bottom tier: $99/mo for 200 contacts
> Middle tier: $249/mo for 1,000 contacts
> Top tier: $499/mo for 3,000 contacts

I sent an email out to the 40 people who registered free accounts on Inlistio. Again, crickets. Of the 40 or so who signed up for free, only 25% of them actually used the free credits.

That first week was off to a bad start, but I kept going.

At the end of August, about a week after the last price change, I lowered prices again; this time by a lot.

Bottom tier: $29/mo for 40 contacts
Middle tier: $59/mo for 100 contacts
Top tier: $249/mo for 1,000 contacts

The first customer came in, finally, about a week after that last price change. It was a $29/mo subscription, but I didn't mind. I was elated. The seal was broken!

It took another two weeks to get the next $29/mo customer and then I had my first big break, a $600/mo customer who had a lot of contacts to track. She paid three months upfront—$1,800— and I texted Max a picture of the receipt. We were both pumped!

But there was a problem. (And by the way, there's always a problem.) The data providers I was using were expensive. Really expensive. I ended up spending nearly all of the $1,800 on servicing her account. That's no way to run a business.

Two months lapsed before we had another customer. In the meantime, while on a Toofr customer call, I had a major insight. I was doing Inlistio all wrong. I didn't need these expensive data providers. There was a much cheaper way to get the data I needed.

I hacked it together and ran the numbers. The cost was 90% lower so I lowered pricing again, one last time, and quickly got two more customers.

Bottom tier: $19/mo for 1,000 contacts
Middle tier: $149/mo for 10,000 contacts
Top tier: $249/mo for 20,000 contacts

I lowered the bottom tier and raised the middle tier, but reduced the effective price per contact across the board by as much as 90 percent. Since most marketers have large lists, closer to 10,000 contacts, it makes it a lot easier to attract them. I used to need to charge $1,000 for a list of that size. Now I can do it for a tenth of that amount.

Be warned, though, that lowering prices is not the best growth tactic. It's been several months since that last pricing change and I've changed my approach again, removing the pricing page altogether and doing custom pricing and demos for interested customers. For those same 10,000 contacts I'm now charging $249/mo with a three-month upfront commitment. I'm attending conferences and getting great feedback.

Each business is different. The only thing that's the same is the hustle required to figure out how to get it making money.

Ad campaign testing

Now let's look at the tactics behind driving traffic to your landing pages.

You'll drive traffic to your landing page experiment with an ad campaign. I recommend using Google or Facebook ads and at least a budget of $100 to accumulate 50-100 clicks.

If you have the funds, spend $100 each on Google and Facebook. I've seen and heard enough stories from professional digital marketers to know that failure on one platform doesn't mean failure on another. Facebook and Google have different technologies, audience parameters, and most importantly, buyer intents.

Google AdWords

Google is the preeminent advertiser on the internet. At some point, no matter what you do as an online entrepreneur, you'll eventually need to dive into AdWords and run a campaign.

AdWords is a behemoth of an application. A deep dive into this technology is beyond the scope of this book but there are dozens of good tutorials and YouTube videos about it online.

Google users are actively *looking for answers*. Consider that when you choose your ad headlines. They should read like answers to a question that your ideal customer has in mind.

Some examples are:

- How do I lower my business burn rate?
- What's the best accounting software?
- How do I pay my contractors?
- Where should I buy my next car?

Whatever the idea is that you're testing, the ad headline should answer that burning question your customer has. It should pop out among the Google results.

The best way to research your ad headlines is to simply do some googling on your own. Ask Google the question your customers might be asking. Become your own ideal customer and dive into Google and see what's there. You'll be surprised how quickly the ad headline ideas will come.

It's a valuable exercise and will not only bring up interesting competitive intelligence in the organic results (the main area below the search bar) but will also give you ideas for headlines in the advertising results (on the right side and immediately below the search bar.)

Facebook Ad Manager

Unlike Google, most users are not on Facebook to get their questions answered. They're passively consuming content, usually on a break from professional business. Facebook's ads are on a column to the right side of the user's newsfeed.

Also unlike Google, and perhaps because of this passive viewership, Facebook allows and encourages you to use images. They'll provide a library of free stock images to use above your headline.

So your goal with Facebook ads is to grab attention. Studies have shown that images with people in them perform best. Rather than answering a question, as I suggested in the Google section, you should be provocative with your Facebook ad headline. You need to pique the interest of a passive viewer, and a compelling statistic or a bold claim is your best bet at drawing clicks.

There are several reasons why both B2B and B2C marketers love Facebook. First of all, its reach is at least as broad as Google's. With billions of users, its potential is limitless. And because of the way it is structured and the user data it has access to, Facebook has much deeper audience targeting than Google. You can be very specific about who you want to reach.

When you combine breadth and depth at massive internet scale, you have an advertiser's dream platform. Like AdWords,

Facebook Ad Manager is overwhelming at first, but you're only a couple of online tutorials away from figuring it out. Dedicate an hour to reading it and clicking through to create your first ad and you'll begin to understand. It's complex but you'll get used to it.

Some general suggestions about setting up your ads

Follow these rules whether you're advertising on Facebook or Google or both.

Like your landing page descriptions, choose wildly different headlines. You can copy your landing page descriptions if they fit or edit them down as needed. You've already done this work so you might as well reuse it.

Again, the headline should be the only difference between the ads; make sure you use the same audience parameters for both ads and the same image on Facebook.

Keep your audience broad. Audience parameters shouldn't be in this experiment yet. Since we're doing a B2B business, a good, broad audience is all adults (21+) in the United States. You'll be tempted to filter down on industries and job titles on Facebook, but resist it. Stay broad while we're just doing headline tests.

If you use Google, then you'll need to choose *keywords*. Facebook doesn't require this. Keep your keywords as broad and obvious as possible while maintaining a low *cost-per-click* (CPC). You should be able to get the CPC around $1. Broader terms cost more because they get more traffic, so be specific without being too verbose. Use verbs. For me, a good just-broad-enough keyword for Toofr is simply, "find emails" and "email finder."

Organize your ads by putting them into an "Ad Group." This is what Google and Facebook call a set of ads that share all the same parameters except the ad's headline and/or image.

Finally, set a daily budget of $20 so it'll take five days for you to use all $100. This way we can wash out any regular flux in internet traffic (e.g. weekends vs weekdays).

With all of that done, we wait and see what happens. If you're using Unbounce or Instapage, you'll see a running total of views and conversions. A day or so after you launch the ads, check back in your landing page analytics to make sure it's working and conversions are tracking.

Funnel analysis

We now have two layers to our funnel. First, we have the ad. The ad links to the landing page. The landing page has a CTA to collect an email address. That's the conversion event.

The full experiment funnel looks like this:
- Ad headline experiment: Ad 1 + Ad 2
  - CTR
- Landing page experiment: Landing 1 + Landing 2
  - CVR
- Email submission

Once your budget is spent, you'll go into the ad manager on Facebook or Google and see a *click-through rate* (CTR) for each ad. The CTR measures how many impressions (showings) it takes to get one click. If your headlines are distinct then you should have one ad clearly outperforming the other.

A high CTR is 5-10%. Usually it's around 1-2%. If you can find a headline that's above 5%, then that's a really good indicator of interest in the headline. If you used that ad headline in a landing page description then I'd be surprised if that page didn't perform well too.

Moving down the funnel, once a visitor lands on your page, the software will register a visit and track how many visitors it takes to get one CTA completion. This ratio is your *conversion rate* (CVR). Since you're only driving traffic from ads, a high conversion rate is 10-15%. Normally, on a mature page against all traffic, a good CVR is more like 1-5%.

So let's do the math. Let's say $100 bought you 100 clicks (that would imply a $1 CPC). Your CPC may be higher or lower, but you should try get around 100 clicks even if it means putting another $20 or $40 into this experiment.

Those 100 clicks will probably get you 10 email addresses, so your entry *cost per acquisition* (CPA—aren't you loving these acronyms?) is $10. That's not a bad CPA to start. You can get it down further by optimizing around the benefits and features that generate the most clicks.

To do this, you should be sure to incorporate the winning ad headlines into your landing page copy and focus the rest of the copy on that particular feature or related set of features. Modify your ads in a similar way, again focusing the ad headlines and copy on those same one or two features and benefits.

Each time you do this you'll spend another $100 to $150 and

be even more confident about building your product.

The true, final CPA will not be known until you launch and can actually start getting customers. If it takes you 100 email addresses to get one paid customer, then multiply the entry CPA by 10 to get a final CPA of $1,000.

I just heard you gasp.

One thousand dollars in ad spend just to get one measly customer? Yes indeed! This is yet another reason why you need to solve a real pain for real business users. If you can get the average customer to pay more than $100 per month, then you're probably at breakeven or better in the long run on that $1,000 ad spend.

Three final considerations

Now that you know how to describe your idea and which benefits to focus on, you need to do a little bit more work before diving into building.

I believe that each of these considerations is merely a gut check. If you believe in your idea and are excited to work on it, then you're 99% of the way there. This last bit of diligence is meant to make sure you're in it to win it.

Technical complexity

How difficult do you think it will be to build? Talk to some engineers you know. Describe the application, what it does, and the one or two features you absolutely need to have in order to launch. If you're not very technical, then being aware at this stage will help you push through the inevitable hurdles that you'll encounter when actually building.

When you do this diligence, still keep in mind the difference between the finished product and the bare-bones "minimum viable product" version, or MVP. Also, caveat the technical complexity with the reminder that ultimately it will be marketing that dictates success or failure. You just need a product that works, so what you're really testing here is how long it will take to build that MVP.

Competitive landscape

Who's already doing this? Don't let yourself believe you're the only one. There's always one or two players dominating and a handful of others playing catch-up.

Don't let your research dissuade you. It's simply awareness so that when a customer inevitably asks what makes you different you'll know how to answer.

If you're not that different in features, then you should be different in price, at least to start. So in addition to looking at a) who they are and b) what exactly they offer, you'll need to pay attention to c) how much they cost.

I also like to check out their traffic and see how they're trending. Alexa and Compete are great tools for this. Flat or increasing are signs that the market is healthy. A declining traffic chart could mean an opportunity for you to enter but could also mean that there's something rotten about the market.

If someone ahead of you is failing, tread cautiously. Try to find out why. I'd much rather enter into a market where my competitors are doing well than one where everyone is struggling.

Market size

Should you focus on a large market or a niche one? Should you choose a problem that everyone has or a problem that a smaller, more specialized customer has?

If you're looking to raise money from investors then you need to have your sights on a big market with a lot of customers. It will be difficult to get investors excited about entering a niche market.

However, the nice thing about running a small business yourself, without investors, is you can enter a small market and do very well for yourself.

What do I mean by large versus niche? An example might help.

Let's say you have a sales background and have always been frustrated with customer relationship management (CRM) software. You think it's too complex, too expensive, just plain too ugly. After reading this book you decide to build a simple, elegant alternative in this category.

The good news is the CRM market is huge! Salesforce is the dominant player and pulls in about $1 billion per month (yes, per *month*) in revenue. Other large companies in this market include Oracle and Microsoft. You can count on every business on the planet needing to purchase this software at some point. This is the epitome of a large market.

If you decided to build a general CRM application then you would be competing against these huge incumbent players. On the one hand, there are millions of potential customers. On the other hand, you have dozens of large and small companies competing with you for those accounts. Large markets are going to be very competitive.

On the other hand, maybe you happen to be a dog trainer on the side and have a great network of other dog trainers in your local community and online. Perhaps you've heard from them how hard it is to keep track of clients, the names of their dogs, which training packages they bought, and whether they prefer to be contacted by email or text message.

Hearing this, you might decide to build a CRM for dog trainers. Typically, niche products cost a bit more because they're specialized and there's less competition. In this case, your CRM features would be optimized for dog trainers and therefore your product would be completely differentiated from both the huge and smaller CRM players. Rather than having to compete online for SEO and expensive ad units, you could advertise in pet magazines and go to dog training conferences. There's less competition but you have to look harder for customers.

Like nearly everything in business, there's no right way to go. I merely suggest you be aware of these pros and cons when deciding whether to go after a large or niche market.

	Pro	**Con**
Large Market	Easy to find customers	Downward pricing pressure due to competition Expensive CPC due to competition
Niche Market	High willingness to pay Cheap CPC due to less competition	Need to be very targeted in customer acquisition

In a nutshell, niche markets will absorb higher prices but the buyers are more difficult to find. Large markets will pay less but the customers are easy to identify.

Whether your product is large or niche simply depends on how many people feel this pain today. Markets will shift. What's niche now may be large in a couple of years, in which case you'll be lucky to have entered when there was less competition. If the dog training market were to suddenly expand, you'd get to ride that wave as the #1 CRM for dog trainers.

Whichever market your idea fits into best, know the pros and cons above because they'll directly impact the speed of traction you get after you launch.

Branding and Designing

AS A GENERAL RULE, DON'T dwell on branding and designing. The marketing side of things will ultimately determine your success at attracting customers. That's the first hurdle.

The worst reason for losing those hard-earned acquisitions, though, is building a product that is difficult to use or simply doesn't work. And if you're outsourcing development, you can quickly spiral down a path of never-ending feature creep and redesigns.

It's best if you can think through the basic set of features, pages, and screens so that you or your development resource knows exactly what needs to be built, where the elements will go, and what the user should experience upon signing up for your product.

That's what I mean by branding and design. I'm far less concerned about how *beautiful* your product is than I am about how well it *functions*. Part of good function is a clear brand and navigation, as well as an obvious purpose for each and every page of your application.

You should consider the cases for both guest users and logged in users. Have a logical process for onboarding, and a clear set of pages for users to manage as much of their accounts as possible without needing to contact you.

These are the steps you'll need to take in order to quickly spin one or two of your ideas into a lightweight sketch of your minimum viable product.

Start by mocking up your application with outlines of UI elements

A mockup is a colorless sketch of your application. It's a terrific way to share the vision you had in the Idea Discovery step with your friends, friendly potential customers, and contract developers.

Some popular mockup tools are Balsamiq and Ninjamock, both of which give a "sketchy" look to their mocked up elements. The point is to not get caught up on whether a box should have round or square edges. That doesn't matter right now so they intentionally make their elements rough.

This exercise will allow you to build pages quickly and help you think through the execution of the most critical features of your application. Doing this now will save you time later as you or your developers begin to actually write the code that brings your idea to life.

At a minimum you should mock up these pages:

- The main dashboard to which your customer is redirected immediately upon signing up. It might be a set of charts, a form to collect more information, or your application's main feature or tool.

- A second or third feature or tool page that is required for your MVP.

- An account settings page where your customers can configure your application to fit their needs.

- A page to contact you if they need help.

- A page to upgrade, downgrade, or cancel their account.

Don't spend a lot of time on fancy registration, login, and password reset pages. Most web development frameworks will have out-of-the-box implementations of these pages. You can optimize these pages further after you launch and start driving traffic to them.

As you mock up the main tooling, really look at it through the eyes of your customers. Often you'll leave out something obvious which will create a stumbling block later on in the development process. Do this mockup in at least two different sittings so you'll come back to it with a fresh perspective.

Most people are able to knock this out in a couple of days. You don't need any software or programming experience. The tools I mentioned above, and any others in this category that you might discover, should be very user friendly. Most of them are free to try and you might find that as a solopreneur you'll never need their paid features, which are meant to upsell teams within larger companies onto paid accounts.

Use templates when you're ready to start designing

Design aficionados will not agree with me. It may not be the right approach in the long run but you can always go back and do a custom design later.

If you search around, you'll find that there are dozens, even hundreds, of professional-looking homepage and application templates. There are some good free templates and plenty of good premium templates that cost anywhere from $20 to $100 each.

I suggest the paid variety for their higher quality designs and to give your application a different look than the rest. You can easily spend days thumbing through previews and searching every gallery on the internet. Resist that urge and pick one that feels right to you with your "customer" hat on. Don't spend more than an hour looking around.

You can also copy the look of the landing page templates you used for your idea testing. If it's already working, don't reinvent it! You'll probably still need to buy a template, but can pick a template that looks similar to the landing page you built and then edit it so they're more alike.

Use these shortcuts for colors and logos

It will also be tempting to spend a lot of time choosing your logos and colors. Don't spend more than an hour on this either.

I like to get ideas other websites in the same industry. What colors do they use? Are they bold and brash or cool and mellow? Do the logos have text, common symbols, or are they completely custom?

Most of the time you can get by with a free color palette from an online color palette generator. Give it a base color and it will create primary, secondary, and tertiary color options for you. Usually it will present a dozen or so palette combinations. Choose one that's attractive to you and is not too far afield from the others in the market you're entering.

You can use a resource like The Noun Project to search for an icon or symbol for your logo. Put it alongside the text of your business name in a nice font and that serve as a perfectly nice logo for your business. It will only cost a few dollars to get the commercial rights for a pre-made icon.

You don't want to risk appearing too bold and deterring customers, so don't deviate too far from the norms in your field. You need to attract as broad a range of customers as possible; some buyers will be turned off if they land on your site and see something too far beyond their expectations. Sure, you may stand out, but standing out doesn't always engender trust and lead to signups.

You can rebrand later when your customers are using your product and you have a word of mouth engine already humming. Companies change their logos and colors all the time.

Even Google, with one of the most iconic and widely seen logos on the Internet, has done it and survived. You can too.

Don't stress about the color and logo. Not yet. If your idea ultimately fails, it will not be because you chose the wrong shade of blue and didn't hire a professional designer to spend a month consulting on a custom logo.

So do the best you can, pick something that looks good to you, and move on. It's time to start building.

Building

IF YOU'RE NOT A SEASONED programmer and are building an idea in order to expand your skills, this may be the longest stage of your journey.

Don't worry if it takes months before your work starts to pay off. Keep learning, keep researching, keep running into dead-ends and walls of bugs. You will break through them and get faster and faster at application development.

If you want, do it yourself. It may take two years to launch this way, but you'll gain a priceless skillset. I can't tell you how valuable it's been for me to learn to program. I literally can't price it. I don't think it's a stretch to say it's *priceless*. The speed by which I'm able to launch and test new ideas, get access to new opportunities, and meet and gain the respect of other entrepreneurs is not quantifiable.

I can say that being able to do it all myself has saved me over a hundred thousand dollars of outsourced development cost in the last several years. I couldn't afford to buy that kind of time, so I wouldn't have launched as many products if I couldn't simply build them myself.

Now I'm going to get a bit technical. It's not important that you understand everything but it is important for you to be aware of the types of services and terms I'm using. I encourage you to read through it carefully even if you're not going to develop your application yourself. You'll manage the developers who do it for you better.

You will eventually need to have an opinion on everything in this section. Some chapters will take you more time than others, and you'll find the best answers simply by getting out there and building. However, I'll describe my thinking so you know what to expect and can develop your own informed opinions.

The goal is not to start just one software company. You should start several, so you're going to choose a set of these services (a "stack") that you can reuse across all of your future projects.

Since I've already used this term, I have a quick note on what it means to be "technical." Here's a checklist. If you answer yes to all of these, then congratulations! I, with no real authority to do so, hereby dub you "technical."

- Do you regularly launch a terminal window to open programs, navigate folders, or check to see why your laptop's fan keeps turning on?

- Do you know what a SQL join query is? Bonus point

if you know the difference between an inner join and
outer join?

- Can you clearly state the difference between an instance
  method and a class method?

- Can you describe why the model, view, and controller
  files are separated in modern web frameworks?

If those questions are completely foreign to you then you
have some reading to do. It will take some time before you can
build a web application yourself. You're not technical now and it
will take you months of active learning or a year of passive learning to become technical. But again, the journey will be well
worth it. The value will be priceless for you too.

If you've read this far and have a pit in your stomach and
want to skip this chapter, I understand. That's okay. You don't
need to be technical in order to succeed as a parallel entrepreneur. This section doesn't require you to be a computer software
geek. Instead, I've written this to speak directly to you and catch
you up on what you absolutely must know in order to outsource
multiple development projects serially or in parallel.

Don't give up yet. Keep reading!

It took me about five years to become technical, and I'm still
probably somewhere between a novice and an intermediate programmer. The thing is, I love the technical stuff. It activates a
part of my brain that really enjoys being challenged. So I eat it
up. Maybe you will too, but don't let that be a barrier. Another
way to learn while still speeding up development is to outsource

it to a friendly expert who doesn't mind answering questions and can teach you how your application works as they build it.

The following questions are extremely important. You should have an educated opinion on these answers in order to build multiple products successfully. It will only help you as an entrepreneur to have a deeper understanding of this side of things.

Let's jump right in.

Where will you host your web app?

Hosting today for companies at our scale comes in two flavors: virtual private servers (VPS) and hosting platforms or platforms-as-a-service (PaaS).

Some notable examples of VPS's are Rackspace, Digital Ocean, and the EC2 product from Amazon Web Services (AWS). They'll give you the ability to log into a server and install everything you need to run your application.

On the other hand, a PaaS will do all the server creation and code deployments for you. The most popular PaaS is Heroku, which is owned by Salesforce and itself runs on AWS EC2. AWS has its own PaaS as well, Elastic Beanstalk, which has many of the same features as Heroku but is less expensive.

	Pro	Con
VPS	Have complete control over server environment. Run everything on a single server. Cheapest options start at $5-10/mo.	Requires another skillset: UNIX/Bash commands. Have to maintain and continuously install patch updates. Prolonged downtime if a server fails. Deployments can be complex.
PaaS	App can be created and deployed in minutes (seconds even). Server maintenance and updates are taken care of. Can serve basic applications for free and then starts around $15-20/mo. Code repository is included.	Little to no customization of server environments allowed. Not ideal for cutting-edge technology. Can be costly at high scale—3-4X more expensive than VPS.

Recommendation: Heroku. It's free to start and scales at low cost. If you're not technical then I don't recommend using a technology that Heroku doesn't support. Disregard the buzz about the latest, greatest thing. Use a tried and true software that's already supported by Heroku.

Which language will it be written in?

Your options are many, but the three that you should choose from are Ruby, Python, and JavaScript. If you're paying any attention to technology then those three names should sound familiar.

Python + Django

Python is about thirty years old. It began in academia and became popular because of its semantic and descriptive language. If you've seen code snippets in the past, you probably saw a bunch of parentheses, curly brackets, and semicolons. Python got rid of those and people rejoiced.

It became popular among data scientists and today, for example, the code written to analyze electron collisions at the Large Hadron Collider in Lucerne, Switzerland, is written in Python. Most of the machine learning community still uses Python, and blockchain developers have also embraced it. It has a large community of engineers who write and release free, open-source packages of code, called libraries, which give Python a suite of out-of-the-box tools to use in your programs.

One of those libraries is Django and it has become the *de facto* way to build modern websites using Python. If you're going to develop your app in Python, you're going to use the Django library to do it.

Ruby + Rails

Ruby is a more recent language, developed in Japan as an alternative to Python about 20 years ago. It's also very easy to read; many would argue more so than Python.

Ruby began as a very niche, almost underground movement to fix some of the things that bothered programmers about Python. Then everything changed when a Danish developer named David Heinemeier Hansson began to write a Ruby library (they're called gems in Ruby) for web development. He named the gem Rails and the project became known as Ruby on Rails.

Ruby on Rails is the most popular web programming language with millions of websites built on it. Its most recent release, Rails 5, went live in spring 2017 to much fanfare in the Ruby community. It's a major milestone for the project and speaks to the quality, security, and longevity of this technology.

If you dive into Ruby, you will find that there is a gem for everything. Not to be outdone, even the super nerdy data and statistics libraries from Python have been rewritten in Ruby. It's a very safe choice.

JavaScript (Node.js) + Angular or React

JavaScript right now is like the Wild Wild West. Only a few years ago it was a purely front-end, client-side (e.g. it only runs in your browser) language. Today there's much excitement around JavaScript itself emerging as an option to run back-end logic, database queries, and of course the cool front-end tricks it's known for.

The difference between JavaScript and Ruby and Python is that: JavaScript runs in browsers and Ruby and Python run on servers.

Have you ever noticed that sometimes you click on a button on a website and the page will reload, and other times you'll briefly see a spinning icon and then content will magically appear without the reload? That asynchronous loading is JavaScript in action. It's logic that runs in your browser so your server doesn't need to do the HTML page rendering and cause the reload.

To make this more clear, here are some real examples of both techniques on sites you've probably visited:

Pages reload:
- New York Times
- Wikipedia

Pages load asynchronously:
- Facebook
- Gmail

Unlike Ruby and Python, the JavaScript world is in a controlled chaos state and is moving very, very fast. The most popular website development package (that's a library or gem in JavaScript) is called Node.js. Node is really just a backend package, so on top of Node you'll need any number of front-end packages. The two most popular are Angular (released by Google) and React (released by Facebook).

There are thousands of posts published online about each of these JavaScript technologies. The important thing for you to know is that they exist. I won't go into the pros and cons of each here because that ultimately boils down to a personal choice about the behavior of your web app and your desire to use the latest tech.

> **Recommendation:** Unless you're already technical, use Ruby on Rails and don't attempt JavaScript yet. You can add a slick JavaScript front-end later. Rails will give you everything you need and your code will be efficient and easy to understand. Plus, if you outsource, you will have many inexpensive Ruby development options.

What kind of database will you use?

Fortunately, we're back down to two choices, and I'm just going to cut to the chase here and tell you to use Postgres. You still need to know what the other option is, though.

SQL - Postgres

Postgres is a transactional database, which means it uses tables and rows just like an Excel spreadsheet. It's the most popular kind of database, commonly known as SQL (Structured Query Language). There are competitors to Postgres in the SQL landscape, including MySQL which is now maintained by Oracle, but in recent years Postgres has emerged as the most reliable and fastest of the SQL technologies.

NoSQL - MongoDB

The alternative to SQL is a document-based approach, commonly called NoSQL. The leader in this space is MongoDB. Rather than having rows on tables, you can think of each row being a document with arbitrarily structured data. The documents can still relate to each other but if you want to add a new kind of data, you can just add it. That's the main benefit—no declaring new columns and having to migrate your tables. The new columns can simply just appear.

> **Recommendation:** Use Postgres SQL. It's a much older, safer, and more popular technology. The migration process may seem complex at first but if you think through your application structure well in advance, you won't need to change your tables too much. Your migrations will usually be adding new fields, which is easy to do. Document-based storage simply isn't necessary in 99% of cases.

Where will you store your code?

Heads up! This is critical.

You *need* to use a code repository and you *must* be the owner of the repository account. If you work with third-party developers, then you need to invite them to *your* repository, not the other way around. You must be the owner of the repository.

Even if you develop everything yourself, using a code repository is good hygiene. You don't want all of your undeployed source code stored locally on your laptop. If it gets lost or stolen then you might lose weeks or months of work. Code repositories are remote and work in conjunction with a versioning system like Git. They'll track your code changes (called "pushes") and help you collaborate with others you will want to bring onto your project in the future.

Because it's inexpensive, easy to use, and just the right thing to do, I'll simply say that a code repository is a must-have.

> **Recommendation:** Use GitHub. There are alternatives like BitBucket, and Heroku has a built-in code-repository, but GitHub has a beautiful, intuitive design and issue-tracking features that are worth exploring.

Which design framework will you use?

A design framework is a file in cascading stylesheet (CSS) format that you include in your website markup to streamline the look and feel of your website.

If none of that made sense, I'll explain briefly how a web page works. First, you have HTML, which is the structure of your page and looks like <div>content</div> or <h1>content</h1>. Those brackets (which you don't see when the page loads) surrounding the content (which you do see) forms the foundation of your web page design. A CSS file tells your web browser how those <div> and <h1> structures should look when the page loads.

Bootstrap is a wonderful CSS file released by Twitter in 2011 and web design has never been the same. For solopreneurs it makes your website look decent without doing any extra designing yourself. The design frameworks give you styling for:

- Navigation bars
- Forms
- Buttons
- Alerts
- Modals (JavaScript popups)
- Banners
- And more…

Most importantly, it makes your website responsive to the device viewing it. Have you noticed that some websites look good on your smartphone, with text and buttons that scale with your screen, while others look like a version of a desktop website and require you to zoom in to navigate?

That automated resizing to the screen size is called "responsiveness." Without a framework it would be an insane amount of work to do, and most of us aren't knowledgeable of CSS beyond the basics. Bootstrap takes care of all the heavy lifting for you and it's free.

The two most popular options are Bootstrap and Foundation, with new entrants like Tailwind and others coming up all the time.

Twitter Bootstrap

These days you can't visit a new company's homepage without seeing some of the tell-tale signs of Bootstrap. This is good and bad. Bootstrap is stable and well-documented with a huge community of other developers asking and answering questions about Bootstrap on sites like Stack Overflow. No matter what problem you run into, someone else has also encountered it and posted the answer online. It's amazing how much support there is online for major open-source technologies like this.

The downside is it's very difficult to make your site *not* look like it's on Bootstrap. You can buy templates that use Bootstrap on the backend and include modifications to the core Bootstrap defaults so your site won't feel like everyone else's site, but it's just about impossible to completely eradicate the Bootstrap vibe from your site.

Zurb Foundation

Foundation, because it's less popular, doesn't suffer from the all-too-familiar design rut that Bootstrap has thrust websites into. However, this also means less community support and fewer design themes to choose from.

Zurb is a design agency, and like Bootstrap their Foundation project began as an internal tool which they later open-sourced and continue to update frequently. It is easier to customize than Bootstrap, so Foundation sites are not as easy to identify visually.

Technically, Foundation and Bootstrap are very similar. They both launched in 2011 and have a 12-column grid system along with the standard set of UI elements.

Tailwind

Tailwind is a distinct alternative to Bootstrap and Foundation. Rather than forcing a set of prescribed defaults, Tailwind gives a comprehensive set of utilities that you can combine to customize your UI elements. The result is more class syntax in your views, giving it a more unique feel to your site and an easier way to change it without digging into the CSS source code.

> **Recommendation:** Use Bootstrap. Go with the majority because it will ultimately save you time and give you more options for template purchases. If you're really motivated to give your site a unique look, then use Tailwind.

Should you use a test suite?

All of the major web development frameworks include what's called a testing suite that developers can run to make sure there aren't any glaring bugs before they deploy their code into production.

Testing suites have a unique syntax and present another learning curve to slow down your development. However, they are very effective in eliminating downtime and user complaints from obvious bugs.

The real benefit of writing tests and requiring they pass before deployments comes when you have a team of developers and a complex application. It's difficult, if not impossible, for a single developer to keep all the linkages across application functions running in their head. They may delete or rename a function, figuring it wasn't used anywhere, and accidentally cause the app to crash or stop working. Really good developers make these mistakes all the time.

So test suites were developed to mimic actual application behavior and ensure that the app behaves as predicted in the test.

You can test things like:

- Making sure a page loads with a certain amount of text or a particular form.
- Ensuring that when the form submits, the data is saved and a user is redirected.
- Validating that when a form is not fully completed it won't save and will alert the user.

Test suites are extremely thorough. Developers can test anything: any button, page load, or backend process. They're especially useful to cover the cases where a user's action is not what you intended them to do. You need to make sure your application can handle an unusual action appropriately. This is where most bugs are introduced and the tests do a great job of catching them.

There's even a movement among developers to write the tests *before* writing the code. It's called test-driven development and has a legion of followers. I commend them for doing it, because I personally hate writing tests. However, I've forced myself to do it; and, while on the verge of deploying and thinking I might as well run the tests and make sure nothing had broken, I've caught many bugs.

So tests are effective, but they may not be necessary in the early days of your product launch. Here's a quick chart to summarize the pros and cons of requiring tests.

Pro	Con
Fewer bugs	Slower development
Easier collaboration among developers	
Better code diligence for acquisitions	

Recommendation: Write tests for the core functionality of the app. You don't need 100% test coverage. Settle for 50% or less, so long as the tools that your users will use every time they log in are well covered.

How will you collect payments?

Collecting money, of course, is a critical feature in your application. There are two popular options today, and you should be prepared to make a choice between them.

Don't be persuaded by small differences in fees. Unfortunately, credit card processing is expensive at scale. I wish the fees were flat, but they're not. Whether you're charging $5 or $5,000, you should expect to pay 3% for payment processing. When you hit that $10,000 per month revenue goal, you'll be spending about $300 off the top on merchant fees.

Stripe

Stripe is the younger of the two options and is favored by most entrepreneurs I know. Started by two brilliant young developers from Ireland, Stripe was designed with software engineers in mind.

If you're not a developer then there's no reason for you to know about Stripe, but you've probably used Stripe without knowing it. From huge ride-sharing applications like Lyft to tiny startups, Stripe has a customer list in the hundreds of thousands.

The main benefit to using Stripe is its ease of integration. They continue to be extremely thoughtful about the developer experience. Setting up your business account is fast and automated, and they have a testing environment that exactly mimics production, which is another huge attraction.

Stripe facilitates ACH transfers alongside credit cards, and allows payments with Apple Pay. Another great feature automates the transfer of payments between buyers and sellers in marketplace applications. It's a huge time saver if you're building a marketplace.

Braintree

Braintree is older than Stripe and was purchased by PayPal in 2013. It too began as a developer-friendly payment processor but was soon eclipsed by Stripe on a number of fronts. After the PayPal acquisition, it has caught up in some key areas like drop-in payment forms. Overall it has benefited from its proximity to PayPal.

If you want an easy integration with PayPal and Venmo, Braintree is the obvious choice. There are other idiosyncrasies around proration of upgrades and downgrades of subscriptions and the logging of webhooks, but none of those differences make an obvious winner.

> **Recommendation:** Use Stripe. It has superior documentation and an active community of online entrepreneurs like you who share stories, tips, and techniques. I respect Stripe for not selling to a larger payment company and continuing to focus on making collecting payments a trivial part of the web development stack.

How will you send emails?

A final consideration is which service you'll use to send transactional emails.

Amazon SES

I signed up for Amazon's Simple Email Service (SES) when it first launched in 2011. The emails were blazing fast and incredibly inexpensive at $0.10 per 1,000 emails sent. No other competitors get anywhere close to that price.

Sendgrid

Sendgrid came onto the scene in 2009 and I remember the fanfare around this company at the annual South By Southwest conference in Austin. They followed a similar path as Stripe, building a critical infrastructure piece of web architecture and making it a breeze for developers to work with. The nerds loved them. Sendgrid became a public company in November 2017.

Mailgun

Mailgun is now owned by Rackspace, a large hosting provider that competes with Amazon Web Services on multiple fronts. Due to its simple user interface and emphasis on making developer-friendly tooling, Mailgun is more similar to Sendgrid than it is to SES.

> **Recommendation:** Use Mailgun. I currently run all of my products with Mailgun. With all of these services, the differences really are in the minutiae. Look at all three, discuss with your developer if you hire one, and make an educated choice. The reason I suggest Mailgun is its position in the Rackspace ecosystem and free Heroku integration.

Conclusion: Choose your stack wisely

I went through this technology stack section in perhaps overwhelming detail for one specific reason: if you're going to run multiple internet businesses simultaneously, they need to use the same stack, so choose it wisely.

Having multiple businesses humming at once is enough complexity. Having them all using different technologies is a fool's errand. Don't do it. You should only have to gain familiarity with one service in each of the categories above. Once you're familiar with its eccentricities and pitfalls, you'll be able to more rapidly spin up other businesses that leverage the same stack.

This is the secret to the technical side of becoming a parallel entrepreneur. Each company may look different, but when you peel back the wrapping it's the same technology. I use Heroku, Stripe, Mailgun, Postgres, Ruby on Rails, and Bootstrap for all of my businesses.

I don't deviate because that would slow me down.

Growing

GROWTH IS A LONG GAME. You'll be best positioned to grow if you do a little bit every day, both for your personal brand and your websites' brands.

It's far easier said than done. Everything you've done up to this point has immediate cause and effect. You post an ad and get clicks. You develop a feature and release it. The turnaround times are fast and feel good.

Growth tactics aren't like that. The results come weeks or even months later, and it's usually not one activity that creates the impact. Growth happens when you consistently cultivate it. It's the accumulation of dozens or hundreds of discrete activities.

That's what makes growth so powerful and yet also so frustrating. When you're committed to growth, you're not susceptible to any single points of failure because there *aren't any* single points of failure. Your growth is the cumulation of months and years of work.

Conversely, you also can't count on an any single activity to move the needle. Silver bullet thinking will only leave you frustrated and confused. Don't fall into that trap.

Here are three broad tactics you can do every day to maintain slow and steady growth of your web application.

Cultivate a following

Bryan Harris, the founder of VideoFruit, tweeted, "It constantly amazes me how big of a cheat code having an engaged email newsletter is."

I've experienced this myself but I had to earn it slowly with Toofr. Having cultivated the list over four years of registrations, I now have over 24,000 engaged readers of my Toofr newsletter. I could have grown faster if I already had an email list of my own personal followers. I could have used that list to test landing pages, get early customers, and intros to potential partners.

I now use my Toofr list to foster adoption of my other businesses. My first two Inlistio customers came directly from promoting to my Toofr audience. That's how tactically your businesses can play off each other when you have a following to use as leverage.

A few pointers on using Twitter

It all starts with whom you follow. If you follow everybody on Twitter, then your feed is bound to be a big bumbling mess. If you want to get good at Twitter, then you should probably start over, unfollow everybody, and start following again, very strategically.

Pick a couple of topics that are professionally relevant to you. Going back to the cannabis business example, you might use Google to find the thought leaders in the cannabis ecommerce space. Who are the CEOs and founders of the most innovative companies in that market? Look them up on Twitter and follow them.

Search Twitter for relevant topics and see who's asking the most interesting questions and giving the most thoughtful replies. Follow them. Before you can start engaging, you need to get a higher signal to noise ratio in your feed.

Once you're following between 50 and 100 carefully chosen people, you can begin to participate. Like tweets, reply to the ones where you can add to the conversation. It will take time but people will notice.

Do this for a year and you will start your ascent. Do this consistently for two years and you'll be someone whom others will follow for tips and insights.

LinkedIn is great for business

The news feed on LinkedIn has recently evolved into another must-use platform for thought leadership. Like Twitter, it takes weekly if not daily attention. Anyone can publish long-form articles that will get automatically promoted as notifications to your network. You can also publish shorter-form posts with public comments and likes.

LinkedIn's feed is automatically curated by the people to whom you're connected and the content that they liked. It's a great way to get industry news, updates from professional contacts, and distribute content.

LinkedIn is a major source of referral traffic to all of my companies. I post a regular report on Toofr's growth and finances and try to keep my connections updated regularly about my other businesses as well.

People respond well to it and I can tell it has a cumulative impact. Many people have commented or messaged me privately saying that my posts continually pique their interest in what I'm doing. It's as though each piece of content adds another pixel to an increasingly focused picture.

It's not the rule of 7, it's the rule of 700

With so much competition for attention, not just within platforms but between them as well (Twitter and LinkedIn, for example), Ogilvy's idea that you need to reach a consumer seven times before they'll remember you feels a bit antiquated. Today it might as well be The Rule of 700.

That's the attitude you should have when it comes to building your personal and business brands. Seven hundred LinkedIn posts, seven hundred Twitter posts, seven hundred blog posts. In other words, it doesn't stop. It's not a week-long or month-long activity. It will take you several years to write those 700 blog posts.

Might as well start now!

Start search engine optimization (SEO) from Day 1

Even before you launch publicly, before you actually want to attract customers, and before you have your second page ready:

Launch the homepage.

Pick two or three obvious keywords for your site. Assuming you're not alone in your market, the keywords you optimize for right now should be the ones that show your biggest competitor in the #1 result slot. With any luck, within a year you'll be right up next to them at #2. That's a fine place to be and you'll get your 100 customers in no time.

I cannot understate how important it is to start your SEO campaign as early as possible. I mean this literally. As soon as you can put up a homepage, do it and be smart about the words on that page. You should have those keywords in <h1> tags, in the <title> tags and in your <meta> descriptions.

The thing to remember is the earlier you start, the faster you'll see results and benefit from the free traffic Google will send to you. It's just like what the financial planners say about saving for retirement. The difference between saving in your twenties and saving in your thirties is night and day. The same goes for SEO. Don't wait until your product is developed to get your landing page up. Start building SEO right away.

As bootstrapping entrepreneurs, there's no better price for high quality traffic than free. You can tap into this fountain by thinking about SEO from Day 1.

Get familiar with SEMRush and Moz

SEO, like online advertising, merges data science, website development, and writing. The two leaders in the SEO analysis category are SEMRush and Moz. Moz has a huge following and hosts the leading conference in this market but many people prefer SEMRush. Here's why you need to subscribe to one of these services:

- Ongoing SEO audit of your pages. They will constantly scan your pages to make sure you're doing all the best SEO practices.

- Track your positions over time. Instead getting your search page position manually, let Moz or SEMRush do it for you. They'll dive deep into the results pages, tracking the top 100 results for each keyword.

- Survey the SEO battlefield. SEMRush tracks the organic search positions of your competitors too. It produces a report that shows which keywords your competitors have that you don't. This data forms the basis of any SEO strategy.

Start a blog on your website

At some point you will run out of landing pages to produce. You can only have so much static content on your site. Once you've produced them, optimized them for keywords, and linked to them from elsewhere on your site, you'll need to create more content.

Where do you put it? On your blog, of course. Write one piece a week and syndicate it on Twitter and LinkedIn. Choose your blog post topics using your SEO reports. Do it regularly, and over time (months not weeks, remember?) you will see the results.

If writing isn't your thing, you can easily hire a writer to do it for you. You can work with one directly if you're willing to go through the hiring process on a site like Remoteok.io or you can use a service like Scripted and have the process managed for you. There's no right or wrong way to do it. Just get it done.

Contact new prospects via email

Organic traffic is the best traffic, but a close second is email marketing. Cold email marketing has believers in every industry and at every stage of business.

If you're new to the idea of marketing to people you don't know by email, it's not as difficult or as sketchy as you might initially think.

In the early days of each of my businesses, I reach out to people, directly and one-on-one, without the use of software. I pick people on LinkedIn who match my ideal customer profile and use Toofr to get their email addresses.

I then craft a message that directly speaks to their business. I do a fair amount of research on both them and their company. This process doesn't scale but it does help me develop a template that I can use at scale. When I first start, though, I begin with a blank slate.

Every business that uses email marketing will ultimately need fresh content written from the ground up. You can google for top performing email templates and pick out some patterns you might incorporate, but there's no one-size-fits-all here. If you want to maximize the opportunity in this channel, do the legwork and build a template one email at a time.

When you do decide to scale it, there are a bunch of services that will help. Companies like Gmass, PersistIQ, Sendbloom, and YesWare plug right into your Google Mail account and will send your templates at regular intervals, allowing you to follow up automatically with your prospects if they don't reply. When they do reply, because these services are tapped into your inbox, your prospects will get pulled out of the sequence automatically.

It's a wonderful way to grow your business and get some early momentum. I stand by the technique and you won't have problems so long as you follow these rules:

- Don't misrepresent yourself or your product.
- Include a functioning unsubscribe link.
- Be targeted, concise, and respectful.

If you follow these rules, when a prospect declines your offer, they'll do so politely and thank you for reaching out. The positive replies will be elated. They'll say they just walked out of a meeting about this problem and then your message came down from the heavens and landed in their inbox.

Like SEO, email marketing has a cumulative effect. You'll want to continually refine your sequences (commonly called "drip campaigns") and subject lines to maximize open and response rates.

You should start email marketing as soon as you have a functioning registration form. If you send a dozen messages a day then you should see results within a week or two.

Maintenance

BUILDING, IRONICALLY, IS EASIER THAN maintaining. When you build, you build for the average user, the one who passes all the tests you wrote. But if your app hits any kind of scale, there will be cases you never considered. Your app will break, and you need to have a plan for how to fix it.

Let the maintenance games begin!

Maintaining Toofr is my single most time-intensive activity. The application can break from user inputs, bad code pushes, and hardware outages. When that happens, I have to drop everything I'm doing and fix it. Those days are distracting at best and completely wasted at worst.

As you add more websites to your portfolio, the maintenance needs expand as well, and there can be serious consequences. What if you have two apps crashing at once?

Record feature requests and low-impact bugs to stay organized

Use Trello, an online organizing tool that uses cards and lists, to maintain your roadmap, record bugs, and save new SEO ideas. It helps to have it all in one place.

Whatever tool you use, return to it consistently. It's very easy to lose track of priorities, especially when you add the complexity of multiple companies at once.

The issues you find in one project foreshadow issues you'll have on other projects. It's a best practice to make the same improvement on all of your applications even if only one is having problems.

The same goes for SEO strategies. It's easy to forget, and it's not any more mental work to make the same edit on the same file in another project. Do it and the payoffs multiply.

Use a customer relationship management (CRM) app to keep track of prospects and customers

Using CRM is also good data hygiene. If you ever bring a sales rep or marketer onto your team, giving them access to a database of every customer conversation you've had will help them get up to speed quickly and help you coach them.

The critical feature of modern CRMs is you can give them access to your inbox. The CRM will record your customer conversations for the rest of your team to see. If you're not comfortable with that level of access, you can also BCC an email address and have the conversations recorded. This way the CRM will only see what you want it to see.

When you're dealing with longer sales cycles and managing multiple conversations, a CRM is the only way to make sure you don't drop the ball. If you tell someone you'll get back to them in a week, you need to do that. Your CRM can remind you, show the conversation history, and track your progress to closing your next big deal.

Schedule time each week for your projects and stick to the calendar

Don't let any one project fall into disrepair. You need to maintain a Trello board, spreadsheet, or some other note-taking system for each one of your projects. Focus on each one at some point every week, even when they don't seem to need it.

This tactic will refresh your memory on the status of the project and helps you to draw connections to that project and ideas you might read on Twitter or LinkedIn. The best way to continually innovate is to find ways to apply the insights of others to your own businesses.

Put critical processes into a background processor and use a crash reporting system

A *background processor* is a service common to web applications. You can design your application so that it throws certain processes into a queue. If the process fails due to a bug in your code or an outage from a data provider to which you're connecting, or any other reason, the background processor will keep retrying it.

If your background processor has a lot of retries in its queue, you can look at the logs, find the problem or bug, and fix it; and when the processor tries again, it will go through. Customers are happy because their requests aren't lost, they're just delayed. You don't need to tell them to go back to a page and try again. Often they won't know there was a problem.

Similarly, a crash reporting system will listen to your logs for major problems and report them to you. My favorite in this category is a service called Sentry.io. It tracks application crashes, gives helpful bug reports including what line of code caused the error, and shows which users were impacted.

Sentry covers the problems that aren't collected in the background processor. Instead of telling every user, including unaffected users, about the problem, you can email only those who were impacted. Customers usually appreciate the proactive outreach.

Respond to all customer support inquiries within 12 hours

Finally, a related tactic and one that I think every solopreneur should commit to, is responding to support inquiries within 12 hours.

Your customers are critical. Every single customer matters and responding to them promptly demonstrates that level of importance.

It's not hard to respond to customers immediately. I put my phone number on every email. I have a chat feature on my site that pings me directly. It can sometimes be distracting but earning a new customer or preventing a churned customer is worth it.

To grow a business, find financial and personal freedom, and one day sell it for a huge profit, then treat every customer with respect.

14

How and When to Sell a Business

HERE'S AN UNCONVENTIONAL SUGGESTION: YOU should always have a number in mind.

The goal of the parallel entrepreneur is not to take a company public. It's probably not even to raise money. Your goal is to grow and then graduate your business into someone else's hands. After you sell your business, you keep building more.

To make your exit as smooth and fast as possible, you need to do the following from Day 1:

- Make everyone who works with you sign a PIIA. Failing to do this can kill a deal.
- Track your expenses carefully and diligently. Clean books make a clean sale.
- Keep your files organized. Everything you sign needs to

be saved! Every contract, employment or contractor agreement, and partnership deal.

- Comment your code as much as possible while you're writing it, and also have as much test coverage as is reasonably possible.
- Keep your CRM updated. An acquirer will want your CRM too and may pay a premium for a well-kept archive of all your customers, prospects, and related conversations.

While you may not be motivated to build your business to sell it, you're going to need an exit strategy if you want to continue on your path as a parallel entrepreneur. An exit strategy will give you a framework for deciding when to let go of a business to make room for a new one.

There's a strong market for profitable B2B software businesses. Exactly the kind of business I described in this book. There's a growing number of investors, entrepreneurs, and private equity firms seeking to buyout sub-million-dollar-revenue businesses. I've spoken to a lot of them, and turned down offers to buy Toofr in a few cases. In the process I've learned there are a few things they all look for.

Keep your margins steady and as high as possible

High margins indicate a healthy business. The people who buy small profitable B2B software businesses expect to see margins in the 85% range. Fight your way there if you're not there already.

Negotiate lower variable costs. Be creative if you can and be brutal if you have to. The financial benefits will be well worth it.

If you can't keep your monthly growth steady, be sure to keep your quarterly growth consistent. Acquirers love to see "up and to the right" charts in your income statement. When you have high margins and growing revenue, you can expect to get 3-4X multiples on your revenue. So For example, if you're making $30,000 per month, $360,000 per year, and your margins are 85% and you have consistent growth, you can sell for over $1 million in cash.

That's the reward for running a tight little business. It's important to keep this in mind as you build and grow. It's also why SEO is so important. An easy way to grow your business is to grow traffic, and the way to grow traffic is to rank on a larger set of keywords.

Have a number in mind

*"I've never met a founder who regretted selling his business, but I've met plenty who regretted **not** selling."*

— **A friend who works in private equity**

Pick a number that would be a meaningful exit. It might be what you have left on your mortgage, or your parent's mortgage, or the cost of your childrens' college expenses. Whatever that number is, that's your number. As soon as you can sell your business for that number, sell it.

Don't get greedy and hold out for a higher offer. You can and should try to fetch as high a price as possible, but if you land at or above your number, then you need to take it.

Don't worry about seller's remorse. You're a parallel entrepreneur. You can and will spin up another business. Or two, or three. You're going to do this again, so don't think about what might have been. Be elated that you took a business from the ground and built it up, extracted a living out of it for a while, and then sold it for a profit, allowing you to start a new business.

Parallel entrepreneurs love to build. That's why you're doing this. In order to keep building, you have to let some businesses go. Some will never make it, and you'll shut them down. Others will do really well, and you'll sell them. After you sell them, you may have the resources to buy businesses with product market fit so you don't need to start them from scratch.

Nathan Latka, an entrepreneur, author, and host of popular business podcast TheTop, says, "It's way smarter to buy a company than it is to start one." For most of us, though, we need to start and sell a business before we can afford to buy one.

That's the beautiful cycle of building, running, and selling businesses on the internet.

15

Conclusion

THE TOOLS AVAILABLE TO INTERNET builders today make it easier than ever to take a portfolio approach to entrepreneurship.

The "side hustle" is nothing new, but the idea that you can have multiple side hustles is new. Internet businesses and automation tools make it possible and enjoyable to start and run multiple companies.

The path to 100 customers each paying you $100 every month is littered with obstacles. Reaching and surpassing this goal may require launching more than one business. Increase your odds of success by being a parallel entrepreneur.

This too is not a new revelation. Investors make multiple investments per fund. They diversify across industries and stages of growth. Entrepreneurs can do that too.

There are a few high-profile examples and countless other lower-level ones. While each founder paved his own path, there are some common patterns.

A typical approach is to start a company while you're at your day job. There are some risks but you can mitigate them by choosing a business that doesn't compete with your employer. Never use your employer's resources for your side business. And read the legal documents you signed when you joined the company. Legal awareness is key.

A riskier approach is to quit your job and then start businesses. It's probably not necessary, but if you must do it, remember that it takes at least 18 months to make a livable income.

Regardless of the outcome, you'll benefit by acquiring new skills that will transfer to your day job. You can explore a new career or make a transition to it, ultimately shutting down your venture and seeking employment at a company similar to it.

The time you put into parallel entrepreneurship will boost your confidence, improve your skills, and ultimately increase your salary, whether it's at your current company, your next job, or by gaining some extra income on the side.

Luck is always a factor, too.

"Sometimes you can do everything wrong and still succeed," Diane Baxter, my CFO when I sold Scripted, told me. "My first startup did over 100 acquisitions. We learned as we went. I've seen other companies that had great teams, great approaches, and it just took too long and the investors wore out and new money was not available."

Some companies, despite having everything going for them, ultimately fail.

It takes a lot of time and hard work, and likely more than one company, to get lucky.

THE PARALLEL ENTREPRENEUR TOOLKIT

PARALLEL ENTREPRENEURS NEED TO FIND every ounce of efficiency available. Software tools are critical, and the best ones are those that let you manage multiple businesses with a single account.

Here's a list of tools that are built for parallel entrepreneurship.

Upwork

The best way to stay lean is to pay only for the help you need. Upwork makes that possible. I have used Upwork (and its previous iterations, Elance and Odesk) at each of my previous companies. I also hired my editor and designer for this book through Upwork. It is built for the modern freelancer and entrepreneur and to be successful with your own parallel entrepreneurship I highly recommend you use it too.

Mixpanel

Mixpanel is best for business intelligence and people tracking. It makes dashboards for critical activities, registration and conversion funnels, and even sends email messages to users. It's the best $150 you can spend each month, especially because you can share the same paid account across all of your businesses.

Heroku

In addition to being my preferred hosting platform for its reliability and ease of use, it's also perfect for parallel entrepreneurs. Not only can you host multiple businesses on a single account, the free hosting accounts are quite generous. You can spin up a website and let it build SEO for months or years—for free.

GitHub

GitHub is an online code repository that has become a cornerstone of the internet development community. It is well-documented, reliable, and inexpensive to safely store the code for all of your websites. Since you'll need a repository for each business, and GitHub was always designed to have multiple repositories per account, it's literally built for parallel entrepreneurship.

Stripe

Stripe is best for payment processing and also lets you view multiple business dashboards without having to log in and out of different accounts. It's built for the modern parallel entrepreneur.

Scripted

Scripted released a product for a single entity to manage multiple Scripted accounts and this makes it a great tool for agencies as well as parallel entrepreneurs. I'm a co-founder of this company, so of course I stand behind both the quality of the writing and its tooling to manage multiple businesses at once.

Trello

Trello also makes it easy to create multiple boards. You can create a board for each of your businesses and easily toggle between them. You'll probably keep Trello open in your browser all day.

Facebook for Business

The agency features in Facebook are perfect for parallel entrepreneurs. You'll create a single business account and then assign multiple pages and ad accounts to that business account. This makes it easy to manage the ad campaigns in a single place for all of your businesses.

G Suite: Gmail, Google Analytics, Google AdWords

G Suite is built for multiple businesses, and because most entrepreneurs have a personal Gmail account and a business account on Google Apps, they've also made it easy to toggle between accounts without needing to log out of anything.

Segment

Segment is useful for managing all of your on-page JavaScript libraries from companies like Mixpanel and Google. Their interface is intuitive and easy to manage multiple businesses at once.

Quickbooks

By making it easy to toggle in between separate business accounts or run a single set of books with classes for each business, QuickBooks belongs on your toolbelt.

Unbounce

Unbounce is a great landing page generator. You can add multiple domains to your account, allowing you to host landing pages for all of your businesses on one account.

Apple Mail & Apple Calendar for MacOS

Instead of G Suite, you might also consider Apple Mail and Apple Calendar. Because email is such an ongoing need, constantly toggling between four Gmail tabs for your email may not work well. Apple Mail aggregates the messages from multiple G Suite accounts into a single inbox and associates the correct sending email on replies.

Similarly, Apple Calendar aggregates all of your business calendars into a single view. It's another big time saver.

HubSpot CRM

There aren't any CRMs that allow you to aggregate data from multiple accounts, unfortunately. HubSpot will allow you to create a CRM for each of your businesses for free. You'll need to log in and out of each one, though.

There isn't currently a CRM for parallel entrepreneurs. A business opportunity, perhaps? Go for it!

ACKNOWLEDGMENTS

FIRST AND FOREMOST, I WANT to thank my mom. This is the only section in the book that she hasn't read and edited. If these acknowledgments are published with any typos, that's why.

I am also grateful to my wife for being supportive throughout this process. I've wanted to write a book for a while and like starting a business or a family, there's no perfect time to do it. She knows this too and supported me starting this project when our youngest daughter was just a few months old.

I must thank the many entrepreneurs I spoke with by phone, via email, and who completed the survey I referenced extensively in this book. In no particular order they are Bruce Katuna, Nathan Latka, Andrej Danko, Buddy Arnheim, Diane Baxter, Kyle Duck, Max Altschuler, Tristan Pollock, Matt McGarvey, Ted Chan, Sheel Mohnot, Jack Spilberg, Berna Haws, Nemo Chu, David Hauser, Josh Pigford, Jonathan Siegel, Michael Lovitch, and Nico Kurlas.

Chris Cole designed the book cover elements and parallel entrepreneur infographics. His website is *chrisandstuff.com*. Elena Reznikova completed the book cover and interior page layout. Her website is *DTPerfect.com*.

Thomas Hauck did my final editing. His website is *bookeditorhauck.com*. I also want to thank Toby Lester for providing initial feedback on the manuscript and assuring me that it was not a complete disaster and Tara Caguiat for doing a first pass on all the typos. I must also thank Jake Kring, my friend and fellow parallel entrepreneur who helped me write my first python script, for catching a few more typos just before going to print.

Finally, I want to thank the thousands of technologists who release and contribute to the open-source software projects that make it possible for people like me to sell software subscriptions for a living. These are the unsung heroes of the internet age.

Without them, online entrepreneurship would be much more difficult and specifically the parallel entrepreneurship I described in this book would be impossible.

Made in the USA
Coppell, TX
12 October 2020

39724453R00116